Improving Your Serve
The Art of Unselfish Living

BIBLE STUDY GUIDE

From the Bible-teaching ministry of

Charles R. Swindoll

INSIGHT FOR LIVING

These studies are based on the outlines of sermons delivered by Charles R. Swindoll. Chuck is a graduate of Dallas Theological Seminary and has served in pastorates for over twenty-two years, including churches in Texas, New England, and California. Since 1971 he has served as senior pastor of the First Evangelical Free Church of Fullerton, California. Chuck's radio program, "Insight for Living," began in 1979. In addition to his church and radio ministries, Chuck has authored twenty books and numerous booklets on a variety of subjects.

Chuck's outlines are expanded from the sermon transcripts and edited by Bill Watkins, a graduate of California State University at Fresno and Dallas Theological Seminary, with the assistance of Bill Butterworth, a graduate of Florida Bible College, Dallas Theological Seminary, and Florida Atlantic University. Bill Watkins is presently the director of educational resources, and Bill Butterworth is currently the director of counseling ministries at Insight for Living.

Creative Director:	Cynthia Swindoll
Editor:	Bill Watkins
Associate Editor:	Bill Butterworth
Copy Supervisor:	Wendy Jones
Editorial Assistant:	Jane Gillis
Director, Communications Division:	Carla Beck
Communications Coordinator:	Alene Cooper
Art Director:	Ed Kesterson
Production Artist:	Becky Englund
Typographers:	Trina Crockett and Debbie Krumland
Cover Designer and Photographer:	Paul Lewis
Production Supervisor:	Deedee Snyder
Printer:	R. R. Donnelley & Sons Co.

An album that contains sixteen messages on eight cassettes and corresponds to this study guide may be purchased through Insight for Living, Post Office Box 4444, Fullerton, California 92634. For information, please write for the current Insight for Living catalog, or call (714) 870-9161. Canadian residents may direct their correspondence to Insight for Living Ministries, Post Office Box 2510, Vancouver, British Columbia, Canada V6B 3W7, or call (604) 669-1916.

ISBN 0-8499-8209-X

Table of Contents

1. This study is for "Who, Me a Servant? You Gotta Be Kidding!" chapter 1 of the book *Improving Your Serve* (Waco: Word Books, 1981). There is no cassette of this message.

2. This message is in the cassette series but is not included in the book.

3. In the cassette series this message is given in two consecutive parts. In the study guide lesson we have combined the two messages on giving.

4. In the cassette series this message is given in two consecutive parts. In the study guide lesson we have combined the two messages on forgiving.

5. This message is in the cassette series but is not included in the book.

Improving Your Serve

More than ever before, selfishness has become a way of life. We think about ourselves, watch out for ourselves, and talk about ourselves, and we defend ourselves when confronted with criticism. Ours is indeed a "me-first" generation that finds itself in a confused tailspin, smug and preoccupied with its own needs, yet desperately lonely, isolated, and cold. We are losing touch with one another, running faster even though we have lost our way.

These lessons offer straight talk and solid, biblical answers on how to live an unselfish life . . . how to be a people-helper, how to serve rather than always expecting to receive, how to give rather than striving to get and keep.

It will seem strange, perhaps, because this message is so seldom heard . . . so rarely demonstrated today. But it is desperately needed!

Isn't this what Jesus Christ modeled and proclaimed? Wasn't He the One who said He didn't come to be served, but to serve and to give His life as a ransom? And when He had the opportunity to take charge and do things His way, wasn't He the One who obeyed the Father, serving Him in authentic humility?

My prayer is that you will sense in these lessons an unusual amount of encouragement to improve your serve as you live in and cope with a world that needs these messages more than ever in history.

Chuck Swindoll

Putting Truth into Action

Knowledge apart from application falls short of God's desire for His children. Knowledge must result in change and growth. Consequently, we have constructed this Bible study guide with these purposes in mind: (1) to stimulate discovery, (2) to increase understanding, and (3) to encourage application.

At the end of each lesson is a section called *Living Insights.* There you'll be given assistance in further Bible study, thoughtful interaction, and personal appropriation. This is the place where the lesson is fitted with shoe leather for your walk through the varied experiences of life.

It's our hope that you'll discover numerous ways to use this tool. Some useful avenues we would suggest are personal meditation, joint discovery, and discussion with your spouse, family, work associates, friends, or neighbors. The study guide is also practical for church classes and, of course, as a study aid for the "Insight for Living" radio broadcast. The individual studies can usually be completed in thirty minutes. However, some are more open-ended and could be expanded for greater depth. Their use is flexible!

In order to derive the greatest benefit from this process, we suggest that you record your responses to the lessons in a notebook where writing space is plentiful. In view of the kinds of questions asked, your notebook may become a journal filled with your many discoveries and commitments. We anticipate that you will find yourself returning to it periodically for review and encouragement.

Bill Watkins
Editor

Bill Butterworth
Associate Editor

Improving Your Serve

The Art of Unselfish Living

Who, Me a Servant?
You Gotta Be Kidding!
Selected Scripture

Today the word *servant* often conjures up images of a person who is ignorant, mistreated, crushed in spirit, and lacking in self-esteem. With this sort of caricature, it comes as no surprise when people scoff at the idea that a leader should also be a servant. But God's Word does not convey this attitude, because it gives us a much different understanding of servanthood—one that is compatible with leadership and even serves to revolutionize what a leader is and does. Moreover, God exhorts all those who have been born into His forever family to become true, biblical servants. So if we are going to obey the Lord's command, then we need to know what a servant is and how we can become one. In essence, that is the focus of this entire series. So let's get prepared to do some real digging. The process of becoming a servant is hard work, and it demands our involvement.

I. A Foundational Perspective on Servanthood

Couched in the grand declaration of assurance in Romans 8 is a brief, yet foundational, statement about what God desires to do in the lives of His people. Read these verses carefully, even aloud:

> And we know that God causes all things to work together for good to those who love God, to those who are called according to His purpose. For whom He foreknew, He also predestined to become *conformed to the image of His Son,* that He might be the first-born among many brethren. (vv. 28–29, emphasis added)

In regard to Christians, God is committed to one major objective: to conform them to the image of His Son, Jesus Christ. What is "the image of His Son"? Christ Himself explained it very simply when He declared His primary reason for taking on a sinless human nature: " 'For even the Son of Man did not come to be served, but to serve, and to give His life a ransom for many' " (Mark 10:45). Jesus' life on

The study "Who, Me a Servant? You Gotta Be Kidding!" is for chapter 1 of the book *Improving Your Serve* (Waco: Word Books, 1981). There is no cassette of this message.

earth was characterized by serving and giving. Indeed, these qualities are inseparable; they are the very essence of servanthood. And it is a servant's heart that the Heavenly Father wants to develop in the fabric of His people's lives—nothing less.

II. Serving versus Ruling

It's easy for us to lose sight of our primary calling as Christians to be servants. This is not a new problem; it also plagued those who walked alongside the greatest Servant of all, our Lord Jesus Christ. One of the clearest records of this is provided by Matthew in his Gospel. There we learn that the mother of the sons of Zebedee came to Jesus and requested that He provide for her two sons to reign with Him in His kingdom—one son to sit on His right side and the other on His left side (Matt. 20:20–21). When the other disciples heard of her request, they became indignant (v. 24). No doubt they were all hoping to have that same position. In response to her request, Jesus told His disciples that they were to be humble servants of one another, not authoritative rulers over each other (vv. 25–27). This same counsel applies to Jesus' followers today. Before we can actualize our roles as Christ's servants, however, we need to realize that there is only one Head of the Church, and that is Christ Himself. Look at these majestic words found in Colossians 1:15–18:

> And He is the image of the invisible God, the first-born of all creation. For by Him all things were created, both in the heavens and on earth, visible and invisible, whether thrones or dominions or rulers or authorities— all things have been created by Him and for Him. And He is before all things, and in Him all things hold together. He is also head of the body, the church; and He is the beginning, the first-born from the dead; so that He Himself might come to have first place in everything.

This does not mean that a church should operate without leaders. Rather, it entails that all Christians, including pastors and leaders, function with a servant's heart—an attitude of serving and giving instead of ruling and taking.

III. Paul: Servanthood Modeled

Besides Jesus Christ, perhaps the finest model of a servant was the Jewish-Christian apostle named Paul. He began many of his letters with phrases that described himself as a servant of God (see his opening remarks in Romans, Philippians, and Titus). He also exemplified the marks of a servant in numerous ways, all of which can be classed under three categories.

2

A. Transparent humanity. In 1 Corinthians 2:1–3 Paul wrote,
And when I came to you, brethren, I did not come
with superiority of speech or of wisdom, proclaiming
to you the testimony of God. For I determined to
know nothing among you except Jesus Christ, and
Him crucified. And I was with you in weakness and
in fear and in much trembling.

Was Paul just being modest? No, he was being quite honest,
transparently honest. Just look at what the popular assessment
of Paul was: " 'His letters are weighty and strong, but his
personal presence is unimpressive, and his speech contempt-
ible' " (2 Cor. 10:10). Paul wasn't perfect, and he openly admitted
it. Like Paul, a servant doesn't try to hide his or her humanity
but lays it bare when appropriate for others to see.

B. Genuine humility. Paul expressed this quality of
servanthood in these words: "And my message and my preaching
were not in persuasive words of wisdom, but in demonstration
of the Spirit and of power, that your faith should not rest on the
wisdom of men, but on the power of God" (1 Cor. 2:4–5). Paul
readily admitted that his preaching was unimpressive. He made
this admission to draw attention not to his own inability but to
God's power to enable. Paul desired that people become
increasingly impressed with the living God and less so with
himself. This suggests two revealing tests of genuine humility:
Does the person manifest a nondefensive spirit when confronted? Does he or she express an authentic desire to help
others? The first test involves *a willingness* to be accountable,
and the second, *a sensitive awareness* of the needs and struggles
of others. Both of these features characterize an authentically
humble servant.

C. Absolute honesty. Paul proclaimed that his ministry was
marked by integrity. Consider these statements of his:
We have renounced the things hidden because of
shame, not walking in craftiness or adulterating the
word of God, but by the manifestation of truth
commending ourselves to every man's conscience in
the sight of God. (2 Cor. 4:2)
For our exhortation does not come from error or
impurity or by way of deceit; but just as we have
been approved by God to be entrusted with the
gospel, so we speak, not as pleasing men but God,
who examines our hearts. (1 Thess. 2:3–4)

Ulterior motives, hypocrisy, duplicity, and political games are
not marks of a servant's life. Instead, traits like an openness to
scrutiny, an unswerving commitment to truth, a dedication to

follow through with one's word, and an unwillingness to manipulate others are some of the signs of a life permeated with honesty.

IV. A Challenge

As we embark on this study of servanthood together, let's commit ourselves to be open to God's Word, to be sensitive to the conviction and life-changing power of God's Spirit, and to be honest with ourselves. Only with this attitude on our part will God be able to transform us into the kind of servants He wants us to be.

 Living Insights

Study One ◼━━━━━━━━━━━━━━━━━━━━━━━━━━━━━━━━━━━━

Studying servanthood in the Scriptures will provide the occasion for us to examine passages from both the Old and New Testaments. However, the bulk of our attention here will be devoted to Paul's second epistle to the Corinthians. Let's get better acquainted with this letter.

- Copy the chart below onto a sheet of paper in your notebook. Then skim the thirteen chapters of 2 Corinthians. As you read, look for words and phrases that speak of servanthood. Perhaps the three categories in the chart will help you become even more specific.

Qualities of a Servant
Transparent Humanity
Observations:
Genuine Humility
Observations:
Absolute Honesty
Observations:

Living Insights

Before we go on to the next study, let's take some time to think through these issues in our own lives. *Being real* is the major message of this study. How can God develop within you a serving style? What thoughts come to your mind regarding the three areas that follow?

- Using the headings given in the chart below, write a self-evaluation. Respond to questions like these: How do I measure up? Where could I improve? What strengths do I already possess? Remember: *Be real.*

Qualities of a Servant
Transparent Humanity in My Life
Genuine Humility in My Life
Absolute Honesty in My Life

God's Work, My Involvement
2 Corinthians 2–4

Selfishness characterizes our contemporary lifestyle. We think about ourselves, watch out for ourselves, talk about ourselves, and defend ourselves when confronted with criticism. Yet we live in a confused tailspin—though preoccupied with our own needs, we are continually more empty and desperately lonely. What we need is straight, biblical talk on how to live an unselfish life. This requires that we learn to become people-helpers, concentrate on serving rather than always expecting to receive, and begin giving instead of striving to get and keep. In short, we need to improve our serve the scriptural way. A good place to begin this process is in our own churches. Let's consult Scripture to see what God has to tell us about servanthood in ministry.

I. **Some Background** (2 Corinthians 2:12–16)

Our study will focus on 2 Corinthians 2–4. These chapters are found in the most autobiographical of all the letters Paul wrote. Information about his life and ministry form much of this book's content. And as we shall see, what Paul says about his own experiences and service to Christ will provide a helpful analogy to our participation in the local church, be it urban or rural, small or large. But before we consider some of the principles embedded in this section of Scripture, let's briefly note some important background truths about Paul.

A. **Paul didn't open doors of ministry—God did** (2:12–13).

In these verses Paul recounts, "Now when I came to Troas for the gospel of Christ and when a door was opened for me in the Lord, I had no rest for my spirit, not finding Titus my brother; but taking my leave of them, I went on to Macedonia." While standing on the shoreline of this westernmost section of Asia, Paul says that God opened a new door of ministry for him in Macedonia. We have no record that Paul had ever been to Europe. Perhaps it was the prospect of leaving familiar turf for foreign and unknown soil that made him restless. But God was calling him to leave the familiar and tackle something new. And because he walked through the door God had opened, Christianity took root in Europe and was eventually transported across the Atlantic Ocean to the Americas.

B. **Paul wasn't satisfied to stay in one place** (2:14).

Paul was making known the "sweet aroma of the knowledge of Him [Christ] in every place" (v. 14b). He had already preached and taught the gospel in Palestine, Syria, and Asia, and now God was urging him on to Europe where he would minister in such cities

"God's Work, My Involvement" is in the cassette series but is not included in the book.

6

as Philippi, Thessalonica, Berea, Athens, and Corinth. Paul was not a one-place person. His satisfaction was met by fulfilling God's desires for him to take the good news of Christ to those who had not yet heard.

C. **Paul was "a fragrance of Christ" wherever he went** (2:15–16a). In the midst of the vision, change, and expansion of his ministry, the Apostle Paul maintained that he never lost that fragrance or freshness of new life found in Christ. And for those who believed in the Christ Paul proclaimed, his ministry was the sweet aroma of life. But for those who rejected his message, it was the stench of death. The same occurs today when Christians present the saving truth to others: some will believe and rejoice to everlasting life, while others will reject and rebel to everlasting death.

II. **Four Facts of Ministry to Be Observed** (2 Corinthians 2–4)

Now that we have our bearings, we're ready to draw out from these chapters some significant facts that pertain to ministry.

A. **Implementing change is difficult** (2:14–16b). Many people think that Paul was a strong-willed, ever-ready soldier for God who was always self-confident in whatever task he faced. But this is simply not so. There were times when his knees probably knocked with uncertainty, fear, and a keen sense of inadequacy. In fact, in reflecting on his own ministry and its fruits, Paul asked, "And who is adequate for these things?" (v. 16b). The question assumes that neither Paul nor anyone else he knew was up to the task of ministry—save one. Look back at verse 14a: "But thanks be to God, who always leads us in His triumph in Christ." No one can serve alone, on their own power and with their own resources. But we who are in God's service do not have to minister this way. As we rely on God's power and faithfulness, *He* will lead us triumphantly through the stretching, adapting, adjusting, and squeezing that often come with doing His will. Yet beware—God doesn't always check with us first to see if we would like to accept changes. When He opens the doors of ministry, He calls on us to take up the challenge of change.

B. **Becoming large is suspect** (2:17–4:2). People often become suspicious of a ministry—be it of an individual, a church, a mission, or a parachurch organization—as it expands and moves in new directions. They tend to think that the ministry is changing for the worse, that it's becoming uncaring, self-sufficient, money-mad, manipulative, and exploitive. Unfortunately, this is sometimes true, but not always. Apparently, some people began to view Paul's changing ministry in a similar way. In this letter he defended himself by saying that he and his co-workers were "not like many [others], peddling the word of God" (2:17a). They had "renounced [that is, willfully made a plan to reject] the things hidden because of shame, not walking in craftiness or adulterating the word of God" (4:2a). Instead, they had chosen "by the manifestation of truth" to commend themselves to "every man's conscience in the sight of God" (4:2b). Paul did not want the Corinthian Christians to lump him with those who were ripping people off financially and morally under the guise of ministering the gospel. Surely his ministry had taken some new turns and expanded, but that provided no reason for people to jump to the erroneous conclusion that he had become like many others—a spiritual shyster. The same is true of those in growing ministries today. Becoming large may make many people suspicious, but this need not bring ruin. As long as we stay teachable and caring, we can break down the distrustful image that often accompanies expanding ministries.

C. **Involving people is basic** (3:1–3a, 5). Paul asked, "Are we beginning to commend ourselves again? Or do we need, as some, letters of commendation to you or from you?" (v. 1). Apparently, some people were accusing Paul of exalting himself by traveling around Europe preaching. Paul answered these charges with a resounding no! He was not seeking to commend himself or get commendations for himself from others. Rather, of the Corinthian believers he said, *"You* are our letter, written in our hearts, known and read by all men; being manifested that *you are a letter of Christ"* (v. 2–3a, emphasis added). The Corinthian Christians were living letters of Christ, not Paul. The Savior, not Paul, was the focus of the ministry. In fact, God is the One who enables His servants to accomplish what they do. As Paul said, "Not that we are adequate in ourselves to consider anything as coming from ourselves, but our adequacy is from God" (v. 5). The Lord is the faithful power source of His servants' competency, adequacy, and accomplishments. If we are to do His work, then we must get off the bench and onto the playing field. God doesn't want ministry watchers—He wants ministry doers. And to have a vibrant ministry, we must all stay in touch with the living God and actively participate in His work. Remember, we who are Christians are living letters of Christ, and we are being read by all!

D. **Remaining servants is essential** (3:6, 17). Paul says that God "made us adequate as servants of a new covenant, not of the letter, but of the Spirit; for the letter kills, but the Spirit gives life" (3:6). Here the Holy Spirit is said to be the Giver of life. In verse 17 Paul adds that the Holy Spirit also brings liberty. People who are involved in ministries that the Holy Spirit empowers experience a wonderful dynamism and vibrancy. Why? Because freedom has replaced legalism. No one is rammed into a corner and impelled to participate, look, and act like everyone else. There is freedom to respond in one's own way.

III. Accountability in Ministry (2 Corinthians 4:1, 7, 16)

Paul mentions two things that we are responsible for: "this ministry" (4:1a) and "this treasure" (4:7a). We are accountable for whatever aspect of God's service we are put into. Our particular ministry doesn't need to be like any other ministry. It can retain its own identity and image. But we who are involved in it should seek to strengthen its weaknesses, build on its strengths, and, through it all, "not lose heart" (4:1b, 16a). We need to forge out the ministry in total dependence on God and with an unswerving commitment to His Word. How can we do this? By realizing that our ministries are dependent not on human ingenuity or strength but on the Lord who graciously chose to establish them.

 Living Insights

Study One ▬▬▬▬▬▬▬▬▬▬▬▬▬▬▬▬▬▬▬▬

If we are to take servanthood seriously, it will demand our *involvement*. We must not sit in the stands merely as spectators, but we must actively get into the game.

- Second Corinthians 2–4 is a passage on participation. Spend a few minutes reading through these three chapters. Copy the following chart into your notebook and begin to jot down words or phrases from the text that speak to you of *action*. Use this chart to aid you in better understanding this great portion of God's Word.

God's Work, My Involvement—2 Corinthians 2–4		
Verses	Action Words	Personal Thoughts

Continued on next page

Living Insights

As you would expect, we will place heavy emphasis on *personal application* in this series. The following suggestions are for your own interaction. Choose one or try them all. The key is to apply these truths to your life!

- Memorize 2 Corinthians 2:14. Ask yourself, Is this my response to God's leading in my life? If not, think through an action plan to adopt this attitude. It's important to have this "servant's attitude" from the start.

- Are you a spectator or a participant? Discuss this with someone who knows you well. Talk about not only what you do but why you do it. Close by asking God to show you some possibilities for involvement.

- What can you do in the next twenty-four hours to demonstrate the attitude of a servant? Think through this question and then act upon your answer. Becoming immediately involved in this way will help you overcome initial fear, apathy, or resistance.

A Case for Unselfishness
Genesis 2–3, Mark 10, Philippians 2

As strange as it may seem, your worst enemy is with you wherever you go. Even when you go to church, he follows. He has sung hymns, read the Scriptures—even bowed his head and prayed right along with you. Yet he hasn't sat in front of you or behind you or beside you. Instead, he has sat in your very seat! His name is Self. The Apostle Paul called him the "old man." You have probably cursed and hated him often, while at other times you have sought to please, exalt, and even protect him. He's afflicted with a disease called selfishness, which demands to be satisfied. But it's not incurable; the illness can be treated. However, as a doctor must study sickness in order to learn how to cure it, so we need to examine certain manifestations of selfishness before we can adequately appropriate its cure—servanthood.

I. Relationship of Adam and Eve: Absence of Selfishness (Genesis 2)

In Genesis 2 we find the first biblical picture of human life devoid of selfishness. There we read about the Garden of Eden—a place of unimaginable beauty and perfect innocence. In such an environment, God created a man and a woman and brought them together in an ideal marriage. The relationship they enjoyed is simply expressed in verse 25: "And the man and his wife were both naked and were not ashamed." The Hebrew word for *naked* in this context means "to be laid bare" or "poured out completely." Their relationship with one another was fully transparent; they were open and unguarded in every way toward each other. The Hebrew term translated *not ashamed* carries a reciprocal idea here which means "they were not ashamed before one another." Adam and Eve experienced an innocent, nondefensive relationship. Between them there were no hidden areas; all forms of resistance were lacking. Selfishness was yet unborn. They were other-conscious: each was completely engrossed in the other rather than in themselves.

II. Results of Sin: Preoccupation with Self (Genesis 3)

Then came sin, an event that radically affected all of human history. In direct opposition to God's command, Adam and Eve ate from the forbidden tree (3:1–6; cf. 2:16–17). And when they did, "the eyes of both of them were opened, and they knew that they were naked; and they sewed fig leaves together and made themselves loin coverings" (3:7). The first result of their sin was not rebellion or hostility but a sudden preoccupation with themselves, as shown by their shame over their nakedness. Each immediately began to look out for number one, or, put another way, they became *self*-centered rather than *other*-centered. Consequently, they tried to cover up their unclothed bodies. However, this was not enough. They also tried to hide themselves from God:

> And they heard the sound of the Lord God walking in the garden in the cool of the day, and the man and his wife hid themselves from the presence of the Lord God among the trees of the garden. (3:8)

The very garden that was created by God for their good pleasure, they turned into a sinner's hideout! Then the all-knowing God called out to Adam, " 'Where are you?' " (v. 9), that is, "Why are you trying to conceal yourself?" And Adam responded, " 'I heard the sound of Thee in the garden, and I was afraid because I was naked; so I hid myself' " (v. 10). God's penetrating reply to Adam was, " 'Who told you that you were naked?' " (v. 11a). Until sin shattered paradise, Adam and Eve were so other-conscious that they were completely unaware of their own physical condition. But now that had changed. In fact, when God confronted Adam about his newly acquired self-centeredness, Adam hurled the blame toward Eve and even the Lord Himself: "And the man said, 'The woman whom Thou gavest to be with me, she gave me from the tree, and I ate' " (v. 12). What we see in this account of the first human sin has since been reenacted in countless ways throughout human history. Sin brings with it a preoccupation with self and a withdrawal from a concern for others and from God. Self-centeredness, self-protection, and self-exaltation pervade a life characterized by sin. We all exhibit these traits because we are all sinners. But God has provided a path for change.

III. Realm of Servanthood: Unselfishness Restored
(Mark 10:35–45, Philippians 2:3–4)

After innumerable generations of sinners, a virgin named Mary miraculously conceived and gave birth to a unique individual—Jesus Christ. He was entirely without sin and, thus, completely unselfish. He gathered around Himself twelve sinners whom He chose to personally disciple. Two of these followers, James and John, were brothers and former fishermen. One day they came to Jesus in all of their self-centeredness and made a request of Him: " 'Grant that we may sit in Your glory, one on Your right, and one on Your left' " (Mark 10:37). Jesus first told them that they did not know what they were asking for (v. 38a). Then He directly answered their question by saying, " 'But to sit on My right or on My left, this is not Mine to give; but it is for those for whom it has been prepared' " (v. 40). When the other disciples heard this dialogue, they "began to feel indignant toward James and John" (v. 41). So Jesus called the twelve disciples to come closer to Him. After they had done so, He began to give them some illuminating counsel on servanthood. Let's listen to His instruction:

"You know that those who are recognized as rulers of the Gentiles lord it over them; and their great men exercise authority over them. But it is not so among you, but whoever wishes to become great among you shall be your servant; and whoever wishes to be first among you shall be slave of all. For even the Son of Man did not come to be served, but to serve, and to give His life a ransom for many." (vv. 42–45)

The world's system works through intimidation, abusive power, and self-centered drive. But God's people are not to operate this way. They are to live the lives of servants, sacrificing themselves and their possessions for others just as Christ, the Son of God who became the Son of Man, did. The Apostle Paul summarized this timeless teaching well when he wrote, "Do nothing from selfishness or empty conceit, but with humility of mind let each of you regard one another as more important than himself; do not merely look out for your own personal interests, but also for the interests of others" (Phil. 2:3–4). *Selflessness*—that's the cure for the disease of selfishness. And we can only begin to appropriate it through personal trust in Jesus Christ as Savior.

IV. Road of Servanthood: Traits of Selflessness

At least three things characterize a servant of the Lord. In some of the following lessons, we shall examine these and other qualities more thoroughly. But for now, it is enough for us to understand that servants of Christ must be known by selfless traits.

A. Giving. A servant unveils himself or herself rather than conceals, releases rather than keeps, and views the needs of others as opportunities to give rather than as interruptions to avoid.

B. Forgiving. Understanding, acceptance, and adjustment replace blame and rejection in the life of the Christian servant.

C. Forgetting. When true forgiveness occurs, forgetting the wrong done will naturally follow.

 Living Insights

Much of our time in this lesson was spent in Mark's account of the gospel. This particular portion of Mark 10 is also recorded by both Matthew and Luke. Let's look at all three passages and do some comparing and contrasting.

• Copy the following chart into your notebook. Carefully study the three texts and write in all the similarities and differences that you

13

discover. This exercise should expand your appreciation of Christ's words!

Matthew 20:20–28, Mark 10:35–45, Luke 22:24–30	
Similarities	Differences

 Living Insights

Study Two ▬▬▬▬▬▬▬▬▬▬▬▬▬▬▬▬▬▬▬▬▬▬▬▬

Sin has resulted in a preoccupation with self. These words are uncomfortably true. Let's use our Living Insights to work through some practical responses toward a lifestyle of unselfishness.

• People today still hide their sins and hurl accusations at others. Do you find that these two actions create walls in your particular situation? Discuss with your family *when* they occur and *how* they can be avoided. Caution: Beware of hiding and hurling while discussing them!

• Three important terms were introduced in this lesson: *giving, forgiving,* and *forgetting.* Write down each word and give your own definition to each one. Conclude by suggesting one or two ways you can apply each of these concepts to your life.

• Pause and reflect on how others think of you. Would they describe you as unselfish? If so, give thanks to God. If not, ask Him to help you in this area. With a servant's heart, ask for the strength of the Master.

The Servant as a Giver
(Parts One and Two)
2 Corinthians 8–9

Throughout history there have been a number of non-Christian perspectives which all purport to speak the truth about how we should live. But all of these views revolve around the self. And as we have seen, the self is a demanding tyrant, an archenemy of true righteousness. It will only lead us away from God and a life of real satisfaction. What we need to learn is how to look beyond ourselves and become servants of Christ. In this lesson, we will continue to move in that direction by learning about servants as givers.

I. Isn't There a Better Way?

Jesus Christ replaced the self-centered philosophies of His own day and ours with the other-centered perspective of God: Be a servant— give to others! A passage that presents this divine philosophy well and assumes that it's attainable is found in Paul's letter to the Philippian Christians:

> Do nothing from selfishness or empty conceit, but with humility of mind let each of you regard one another as more important than himself; do not merely look out for your own personal interests, but also for the interests of others. (Phil. 2:3–4)

In other words, we should not let selfishness and conceit play any part in our lives. Instead, we should regard others as more important than ourselves. That involves looking for ways to encourage, support, and build up others. And this requires an attitude of giving rather than receiving or taking.

II. Is All This Biblical?

No doubt about it—a lifestyle of giving is thoroughly supported in Scripture. Many passages could be cited, but a few key ones will meet our needs here. Don't run over them quickly; instead, take time to read them reflectively.

> Not that we are adequate in ourselves to consider anything as coming from ourselves, but our adequacy is from God, who also made us adequate as servants of a new covenant. (2 Cor. 3:5–6a)

> For we do not preach ourselves but Christ Jesus as Lord, and ourselves as your bondservants for Jesus' sake. (2 Cor. 4:5)

In the cassette series, "The Servant as a Giver" is in two parts. Part One comprises sections I.–IV. in the outline, and Part Two includes sections V.–VI. In the book this study corresponds to chapter 3.

For you were called to freedom, brethren; only do not
turn your freedom into an opportunity for the flesh, but
through love serve one another. (Gal. 5:13)

Does all this instruction about servanthood imply that we are
incompetent and inferior? Not in the least! Authentic humility and
an unhealthy self-image are not bedfellows in Scripture. Rather, we
need to make an accurate assessment of ourselves as being valuable
before God and completely dependent on Him. These are key
elements of true servanthood. Perhaps the following passages from
the Apostle Paul's pen will put this in perspective for you:

For I consider myself not in the least inferior to the most
eminent apostles. (2 Cor. 11:5)

I have become foolish; you yourselves compelled me.
Actually I should have been commended by you, for in
no respect was I inferior to the most eminent apostles,
even though I am a nobody. (2 Cor. 12:11)

III. What Are the Basics?

Now that we have a biblical foundation for servanthood, we need to
know what the characteristics of a servant are so that we can begin
to move in the right direction. There are three essential qualities of
a servant: giving, forgiving, and forgetting. We will concentrate on
the first one here and then the other two in subsequent lessons. So
let's turn our attention to the servant as a giver—one who willingly
and generously gives so others might benefit.

IV. How Should Servants Give?

A prime example of servantlike giving is found in 2 Corinthians 8:1–5.
Here Paul refers to a great need of the Christians in Jerusalem and
relates how the Macedonian believers reached out to meet that
need. In this text we can discern at least four truths about how an
authentic servant gives.

A. Anonymously (v. 1). Paul began by saying, "Now, brethren, we
wish to make known to you the grace of God which has been
given in the churches of Macedonia." Although there were
several churches in the area known as Macedonia, Paul didn't
name any of them. Neither did he give "honorable mention" to
any individual. Instead, the churches and persons who gave to
others remained anonymous. True servants give out of genuine
concern, not so that their deed is noticed.

B. Generously (v. 2). We are also told that the Christians of
Macedonia "overflowed in the wealth of their liberality" in spite
of their own affliction and extreme poverty. They didn't clutch
their belongings and take a vow of uninvolvement. Instead, they
gave of their possessions, time, energy, and finances, even when
it seemed they had no more to give.

C. Voluntarily (vv. 3–4). The Macedonian Christians gave because they wanted to: "For I testify that according to their ability, and beyond their ability they gave of their own accord, *begging us with much entreaty* for the favor of participation in the support of the saints" (emphasis added). Have you ever heard of someone begging to help someone else? No one had to hound or force these Christians; they begged others to allow them to participate in fulfilling the needs of others. They did not want to be left out of the opportunity to give.

D. Personally (v. 5). Paul goes on to say that in their giving, "they first gave *themselves* to the Lord and to us by the will of God" (emphasis added). It's impossible to give ourselves to others at arm's length or *in absentia*. Personal involvement requires, first, giving ourselves to the Lord, and then, being willing and flexible to adapt our ways and schedules to fit another person's needs.

V. How Much Does Giving Cost Us?

In Luke 9:23 Jesus summarizes the cost of being His servant: " 'If anyone wishes to come after Me, let him deny himself, and take up his cross daily, and follow Me.' " To be Christ's servants, we must dethrone ourselves and enthrone Him, and we must do this daily. Back in 2 Corinthians 8–9, Paul suggests that this kind of giving will cost us in at least three different ways.

A. It costs a thorough self-evaluation. After Paul spoke about the Macedonian Christians, he turned his attention to the Christians at Corinth. He exhorted them to abound in their giving in the same way they had grown in other areas of the Christian life. To help them accomplish this, Paul sent Titus (8:6–7). Embedded in Paul's counsel are four pieces of sound advice that will help each of us evaluate ourselves better.

1. **Seek the objectivity of another person** (v. 6). We are often blind to our own faults and biased toward our own strengths. To counterbalance this, we need the insight of another person to aid us in our self-evaluation. For the Corinthians this objective person was Titus.

2. **Ask hard questions of yourself** (v. 7). Paul observed that the Corinthian Christians were strong in many areas yet weak in their giving. We need to make a periodic assessment of the many areas that comprise the Christian life and not allow our strengths to divert our energy from working on our weaknesses.

3. **Examine your motives** (v. 8). Paul indicated that the Corinthians' lack of giving raised questions about the sincerity of their love. What we do or don't do often betrays our motives, be they good or bad. But this does not negate

our need to examine why we engage in certain activities, refuse to get involved in others, or struggle in one area while we fail in another.

4. **Deal with your own possessiveness** (v. 9). Because we are all sinners, we are all selfish in varying degrees. That fact often makes it extremely difficult for us to give of ourselves to others. And when we do overcome our selfishness, many times it takes a conscious effort on our part. However, when we as Christians reflect on the cost Jesus Christ paid to redeem us, it will challenge our tendency to keep and hoard. It will also provide an excellent model of the personal cost and the benefit to others, both of which are attached to authentic servanthood.

B. **It costs our determined commitment.** Apparently, the Corinthian Christians had begun to give of their resources but then faltered on their commitment. So Paul encouraged them to follow through on what they had started (8:10–11). It's true that we often begin a new task with zeal and exuberance, but it doesn't take long in the process for the excitement to fade. Yet when it does, we need to buckle down and finish the work we began. The same holds true with giving.

C. **It costs our exercising a bold faith.** Paul lays down the principle that "he who sows sparingly shall also reap sparingly; and he who sows bountifully shall also reap bountifully. Let each one do just as he has purposed in his heart" (2 Cor. 9:6–7a). There is no hard-and-fast rule here about how much anyone should give; it's an individual matter. However, the text does indicate that whatever a person sows, he or she will also reap. And we find here that in deciding the degree to which we should give, we should do so trusting that God will reward our gift according to its measure.

VI. Is It Worth It, After All?

God not only "loves a cheerful giver" (2 Cor. 9:7b), but He says that "he who is generous will be blessed" (Prov. 22:9a). What God says is true. What we need to do is believe it and act on it and watch God accomplish the rest. To be sure, giving is costly, but in the end the rewards will far outweigh the price we paid.

 Living Insights

Study One ▬▬▬▬▬▬▬▬▬▬▬▬▬▬▬▬▬▬▬▬▬▬▬▬

We are never more Christlike than when we are giving. The Apostle Paul used the Macedonian Christians as an illustration of servantlike

18

giving in 2 Corinthians 8–9. Let's explore these chapters in order to discover what giving is all about!

- Let's concentrate on 2 Corinthians 8. We'll look at chapter 9 a little later. After you've copied the chart below into your notebook, turn to this chapter and begin recording the observations you find related to *giving*. Look for key words, phrases, and sentences. You may be surprised at how much you uncover!

Principles of Giving—2 Corinthians 8	
Verses	Observations

 Living Insights

Study Two

We've noted that giving is a primary characteristic of a servant. Does giving characterize your life? Take this opportunity to do some honest introspection in regard to this truth.

- Memorize Philippians 2:3–4. How do you rate in comparison? Are you more concerned about the interests of others or about personal interests? Are others more important than yourself? Try saying these verses as a prayer to God.

- *We are never more Christlike than when we are giving, releasing, and sharing.* Find a time to gather your family and discuss this statement. Develop a strategy and plan some specific actions you can use to make this a greater part of your life. Close with a time of family prayer, each one asking God for strength with his or her individual goals.

Continued on next page

Studies one and two of Living Insights accompany the first part of this lesson, and studies three and four accompany the second part.

Living Insights

Let's continue our look at principles of giving from 2 Corinthians. In this lesson we'll turn our attention to chapter 9.

- Copy this chart in your notebook and continue with the same procedures used in study one of this lesson.

Principles of Giving—2 Corinthians 9	
Verses	Observations

 Living Insights

The portrait of a servant is beautiful, yet there is a price involved. Let's zero in on the aspect of *cost.* Are you willing to pay the price in order to be a true servant?

- Do you have a friend who can help you make a thorough investigation of your life? One who will help you ask the hard questions? Sort out motives? Help you in releasing? If you do, spend some time together this week. If not, ask God to give you such a friend and begin cultivating that relationship. This friendship will be helpful to you the rest of your life.

The Servant as a Forgiver
(Parts One and Two)
2 Corinthians 2; Matthew 5, 18

No one has ever been as greatly offended by more people than God. Yet no one exercises forgiveness more readily and thoroughly than He. The psalmist David wrote, "As far as the east is from the west, so far has He removed our transgressions from us" (Ps. 103:12). This same Lord expects His servants to exercise forgiveness toward others. When they are offended, He desires that they harbor no grudge or seek any sort of retaliation. And when they are the offenders, He wants them to make amends and seek reconciliation. Granted, many times this is difficult instruction to obey. But as we shall see, to do less will eventually lead to a torturous existence filled with bitterness, anger, and guilt.

I. A First-Century Account of Forgiveness

Instead of starting with the theoretical, let's begin with the practical side of forgiveness by examining an actual situation that occurred in the early Church.[1]

A. Exhortation to punish (1 Cor. 5). The Apostle Paul strongly chastised the Corinthian Christians for failing to punish a fellow believer who was actively engaged in an incestuous relationship. Indeed, the Christians in Corinth not only knew of this heinous sin but apparently boasted about their broad-mindedness in their acceptance of this believer's immoral behavior (vv. 1–2, 6). Paul called on them to severely discipline this Christian for his own benefit—even to remove him from their midst (vv. 3–7, 11–13).

B. Call to forgive (2 Cor. 2:4–11). Anywhere from six to twelve months after 1 Corinthians was composed, Paul wrote and sent the letter known to us as 2 Corinthians. In this correspondence, Paul told the Christians in Corinth that the punishment they had inflicted on the immoral believer was sufficient (2:6). It seems that they had followed too well Paul's exhortation to punish him, for they were in danger of overwhelming him with "excessive sorrow" (v. 7b). So Paul called on them to "forgive and comfort" this person and to give reassurance of their love for him (vv. 7–8). To this the apostle added a strong warning: Forgiveness should be exercised "in order that no advantage be taken of us by Satan" (v. 11a). When we fail to administer

---

In the cassette series, "The Servant as a Forgiver" is in two parts. Part One comprises points I.–III.A. in the outline, and Part Two includes sections III.B.–IV. In the book this message corresponds to chapter 4.

1. Outline points I.A.–C. are on the cassette tape, Part One, but are not included in the book.

forgiveness adequately, we leave the door open for Satan to come into our lives and use our unforgiving spirit against us.

C. **Need to repent** (2 Cor. 7:8–12). The road to forgiving another person should be paved with an attitude of repentance. This is true not only for the offender but also for the offended party. In the Corinthian situation Paul called on the church to stop punishing the person who had committed incest and to begin concretely demonstrating their forgiveness of him. This exhortation made the church body "sorrowful to the point of repentance ... according to the will of God" (v. 9). In other words, they admitted they had carried disciplinary measures too far and sought to redress the wrong done. In so doing, they opened the way for genuine forgiveness and restoration to take place.

II. God's Forgiveness of Us

The practical side of forgiveness just illustrated is made possible by the theological foundation which undergirds it—specifically, God's forgiveness of us through the substitutionary death of His Son, Jesus Christ. Because we have willfully violated God's perfect standard of righteousness, we have come under His just wrath. Our sin against God has produced a moral debt that we could not possibly repay by our own efforts. But through God's grace, repayment was met by Christ's sacrificial death on a cross. With this He made it possible for God to cancel our debt (Col. 2:13–14). However, the only way we can receive the benefits of beginning with a fresh ledger is to place our full trust in the sufficiency of Christ's death to repay our debt. Then, and only then, will we receive God's unfailing and complete forgiveness. Moreover, when we become beneficiaries of God's abundant grace, we, in turn, have the necessary foundation and motivation to forgive others of their offenses against us.

III. Our Forgiveness of One Another

On the vertical side, forgiveness flows only from God to man. Horizontally, forgiveness should occur between man and man. On this level we see ourselves in two positions regarding forgiveness: (1) as the offender and (2) as the offended. We will look at a couple of passages that address our responsibilities as forgiving servants in a very practical way.

A. **When we are the offender** (Matt. 5:23–24). This text from Jesus' well-known Sermon on the Mount succinctly gives the procedure we should follow when we have offended another person. It reads,

> "If therefore you are presenting your offering at the altar, and there remember that your brother has something against you, leave your offering there

before the altar, and go your way; first be reconciled to your brother, and then come and present your offering."

The procedure Jesus offers here is clear. It has four steps.

Stop. Under the Mosaic Law, a worshiper brought animals as a sacrifice to be slain on an altar before God. This act provided him with a cleansing of sin and a way of open access to God. With the sacrificial death of Christ, however, the payment for sins has been made once for all. Now Christians can come to the Lord in prayer without bringing any other sacrifice for their sins. Jesus' point is that when we come to our Father in worship and suddenly remember that we have offended another person, then we are to stop worshiping. We have other business we must attend to first.

Go. The second step is to seek out the person we have wronged.

Reconcile. When we find the person we have hurt, we need to be reconciled to him or her. That is, we who offend are commanded to initiate a process that will result in a positive change in the relationship between ourselves and the one we have wounded. This requires that we confess wrong, express our grief over it, and seek forgiveness from that individual.

Return. When the first three steps have been accomplished, we are then free to return to God in worship.

This process may raise the following questions that need to be answered. For your benefit, let's personalize them.

1. **"What if he or she refuses to forgive me?"** If this occurs, recall these words of wisdom from Proverbs: "When a man's ways are pleasing to the Lord, He makes even his enemies to be at peace with him" (16:7). You're responsible to do what is right in a humble, loving way. It may take time, but God will honor your efforts.

2. **"What if the situation only gets worse?"** The person you have offended may have built up a great deal of bitterness toward you. So when you go to that individual and try to make amends, you may dissolve some bitterness as well as expose some guilt. This can easily lead to worse feelings and an even less favorable situation. But don't allow this possibility to deter you from seeking reconciliation. God *can* work in a circumstance like this. However, many times it does take longer for the healing process to occur. So go prepared for the worst, but don't fail to go!

3. **"What if I confess my offense to God only?"** Then you would be contradicting Jesus' command to go first to the

person you offended, then second to the Source of forgiveness, our gracious Lord. If you want God to forgive you of your sin against another person, then you must first go to that person and attempt to make things right between yourselves. Nothing else will do!

4. **"What if the person I offended died before I could seek reconciliation?"** Since you can't contact a dead person, find another individual whom you can trust and honestly tell him or her about your offense against the now deceased person. Then pray with this friend for the forgiveness you need from our all-good Lord.

B. When we are the offended (Matt. 18:21–35). Just as there will be times when we have hurt someone else, so there will be occasions when someone will wrong us. In this section of Matthew's Gospel, Christ instructs us regarding our responsibility when we are offended.

1. **Boundless forgiveness: The answer** (vv. 21–22). One of the disciples, Peter, came to Jesus and asked Him if he should forgive sevenfold a person who sinned against him. Jesus answered Peter, " 'I do not say to you, up to seven times, but up to seventy times seven.' " In other words, when we are wronged, we're to forgive our offender an unlimited number of times. Just as God's forgiveness toward us has no boundaries, so our forgiveness of each other should be boundless.

2. **Boundless forgiveness: An illustration** (vv. 23–34). Jesus graphically portrayed His teaching through the parable revealed in these verses. He spoke of a wealthy king " 'who wished to settle accounts with his slaves' " (v. 23b). One of his slaves owed him ten thousand talents. Since a talent was probably worth a measure of gold between fifty-eight and eighty pounds, we can see that the slave was indebted to the king for several million dollars. But because the slave could not repay the debt, the king commanded that he and his wife, children, and possessions all be sold in order to recover as much of the debt as possible. The slave humbled himself before his king and begged to be granted more time to repay the money owed. The slave's entreaty moved the king to compassion, so he released him and " 'forgave him the debt' " (v. 27). Later, however, this slave encountered a second slave who owed him one hundred denarii, which is about sixteen to twenty dollars in today's currency and in Jesus' day equaled an average day's wages. This slave was also unable to repay his debt and begged for more time to come up with the deficit funds. But the slave who had been

24

forgiven of such a huge debt refused to forgive this fellow slave for his much smaller one. Indeed, he threw the second slave in jail "'until he should pay back what was owed'" (v. 30). When the king learned what had transpired, he summoned his slave, rebuked him, and gave him over to the torturers.

3. **Boundless forgiveness: Some reasons.** The story Jesus told conveys two reasons for forgiving others. First, *the refusal to forgive is hypocritical.* Just as our divine King has demonstrated maximum compassion toward us, even when we were still rebelling against Him, so we need to do the same toward others. To do otherwise makes us hypocrites. Second, *the refusal to forgive inflicts inner torment on the unforgiving.* At the end of the parable, the king handed the slave over to the *torturers.* This word in the Greek biblical text refers to individuals who plague or torment others. Elsewhere in Scripture it's used in its verb form to speak of a person suffering "great pain" (Matt. 8:6) and to describe the misery of a man pleading for relief in hell (Luke 16:23–24). The use of this word in the last line of the parable makes its closing message quite clear: *When we refuse to forgive those who offend us, we will suffer the consequences of tormenting thoughts, feelings of misery, and agonizing unrest within.*

4. **Boundless forgiveness: The application** (v. 35). Negatively speaking, our failure to be genuinely merciful toward others will result in God allowing our own bitterness and resentment to poison us inside. However, since every negative presupposes a positive, when we do completely forgive those who wrong us, God will free us from our feelings of torment, misery, and unrest. The choice is ours.

IV. How to Make It Happen
There are two directives you need to remember in order to become a forgiving servant.
 A. Focus fully on God's forgiveness of you.
 B. Deal directly and honestly with any resentment you currently hold against anyone.

Living Insights

We are most like God when we forgive. A statement of that weight requires some examination within the Scriptures. Let's use our Living Insights to do a word study of the term *forgiveness.*

- Locate a good Bible concordance. Make a copy of the chart that follows. Look up these words in your concordance: *forgive, forgives, forgiven,* and *forgiveness.* Then jot down the references in the left column. As you look up the passages, write a brief summary statement for each section of Scripture.

Forgiveness in the Scriptures	
References	Summary Statements

 Living Insights

This lesson had two strands woven together into the single theme of forgiveness. There were words to the offender and words to the offended. Let's apply this study by responding to the appropriate category of suggestions.

- If you are an offender, don't allow time to let the offense grow. Go to that person or group of people and rectify the situation. Ask for their forgiveness. Go in God's strength and with a servant's heart!
- If you have been offended, have you forgiven the offender? Have you dealt directly with any bitterness or resentment you are harboring? Are you being tormented because you haven't really forgiven? Take the initiative to clear up this situation. Make your own thoughts right. Don't let Satan get the advantage. Remember, God has forgiven you!

Studies one and two of Living Insights accompany the first part of this lesson, and studies three and four accompany the second part.

26

Living Insights

Study Three ▬▬▬▬▬▬▬▬▬▬▬▬▬▬▬▬▬▬▬▬▬▬

Matthew 18:21–35 . . . quite a story! A slave gets an incredible break, and he turns around and throws a fellow slave in jail for the same offense! There's no question about it—this is a vibrant illustration of forgiveness.

- Let's really zero in on this story. Here are a few suggestions to help us derive even greater understanding from the passage:

    —Read it through in another version.

    —Paraphrase the fifteen verses into your own words.

    —Act it out!

 Living Insights

Study Four ▬▬▬▬▬▬▬▬▬▬▬▬▬▬▬▬▬▬▬▬▬▬▬▬▬▬▬▬

It is one thing to conduct an academic study of forgiveness, but it takes one further step to *personalize* it. Let's wrap up our thoughts on this topic with a few applications.

- Have you recently considered God's complete forgiveness of you? Unhurriedly think through how vast and extensive His mercy has been toward you. Ponder the depth of His grace. Remember: The measure to which you can envision God's forgiveness of you is the same measure that you should use for forgiving others.
- Bring the family together to talk about forgiveness. Ask each other questions like, Are we a forgiving family? Why or why not? Do we know of any offenses we have committed? How about among our family members? Encourage *all* to share in this time. It could be uncomfortable, but it will do much to knit the family together.

The Servant as a Forgetter
Philippians 3

When considering the role of a servant, three specifics stand out: giving, forgiving, and forgetting. Having given sufficient thought to the first two, it's time for us to turn to the third. While there isn't a great deal of material on forgetting in Scripture, what is given is significant for developing authentic, faithful servants. As we shall see, people who truly serve others, who give of themselves sacrificially, are those who do not keep a mental record of all they have done wrong or even of what is done against them. They have learned how to be *divinely forgetful.*

I. An Overview of Forgetting

The human brain is a remarkable organ. It is capable of an incredible amount of work, and it retains everything it absorbs. In fact, it never really forgets anything that has been filed into it. Because this is true, how can anyone ever forget an offense as Scripture calls us to do? Four passages will help us to answer that question. We'll look briefly at three of them and then peer longer into the fourth.

A. Disregarding an offense (Ps. 119:165). Here the psalmist tells us that "those who love Thy law have great peace, and nothing causes them to stumble." He advises us to keep our minds focused on God's revealed will, for as we do, we will experience an abundant peace and be enabled to resist stumbling over offenses.

B. Removing a judgmental spirit (Matt. 7:1–5). Jesus' teaching in this passage brings a crucial principle to the subject of forgetting. Seriously consider His strong words:

> "Do not judge lest you be judged yourselves. For in the way you judge, you will also be judged; and by your standard of measure, it shall be measured to you. And why do you look at the speck in your brother's eye, but do not notice the log that is in your own eye? Or how can you say to your brother, 'Let me take the speck out of your eye,' and behold, the log is in your own eye? You hypocrite, first take the log out of your own eye, and then you will see clearly enough to take the speck out of your brother's eye."

Jesus warns us against possessing a judgmental spirit—an attitude which expresses itself through petty, negative, nit-picking judgments on other people's lives. Instead, we need to focus on our own faults and inconsistencies and set those of others aside. By doing so, we will spend more time dealing with our own logs than with other people's specks—a sure cure for a judgmental spirit.

C. **Keeping no score of wrongs** (1 Cor. 13:5). Here the word "love" in the original Greek is *agápe,* which is a selfless love—like the love God has toward us. This kind of affection "does not take into account a wrong suffered" (v. 5). Thus, a true servant with a heart of love does not meticulously record in a ledger all the wrongs committed against him. In fact, he breaks the pencil in two and says, "I refuse to keep score. I will disregard them."

II. A Closer Look at Forgetting (Philippians 3:7–14)

As we have already seen, to *forget* does not mean to erase something from our memories. Rather, from a biblical perspective, the term means to constantly disregard offenses made against us, to remove a judgmental spirit from our lives, and to keep no score of wrongs that we suffer. But this is only the negative side of forgetting. Scripture also presents us with the positive side, and it is clearly brought out in Paul's inspired words recorded in Philippians 3:12–14. He prefaced these verses by reviewing his own history as a Jew *par excellence* (3:4–6). But he explained that when he became a Christian, the things that were once important to him dissolved into insignificance (vv. 7–8). Knowing Christ and "the power of His resurrection and the fellowship of His sufferings" (v. 10a) became Paul's consuming goal after his conversion. And yet this dramatic change in his life did not yield a new spirit of pride, but a servant's heart instead. Indeed, in verses 12–14 of this chapter, Paul's words reveal three important characteristics of a servant who is able to forget.

A. **Vulnerability.** In this passage Paul reveals this important quality. While looking forward to the day when he would "attain to the resurrection from the dead" (v. 11), Paul quickly added, "Not that I have already obtained it, or have already become perfect" (v. 12a; cf. v. 13a). He knew he would not be perfect until his resurrection. So with complete honesty, Paul could readily admit his imperfection. Paul's openness displays an important step on the path to forgetfulness: We must begin by realizing our own shortcomings and be vulnerable enough to admit them to those around us. We also need to maintain a teachable spirit—that is, the willingness to learn from *anyone* at any time—and be reluctant to appear as infallible experts. All these things are crucial elements in being vulnerable.

B. **Humility.** Paul said, "One thing I do: forgetting what lies behind . . . I press on. . . ." (vv. 13b–14). Paul purposely disregarded the significance of his past achievements (vv. 4–6) and the many wrongs done against him (2 Cor. 11:24–27). In Genesis 37–50 we read of another man, Joseph, who had a past full of bad memories. When he was seventeen years of age, he was sold into slavery by his own brothers. His owners took him to Egypt, to a foreign land, where he was later tossed into prison on a false charge. He was neglected, abused, and mistreated until, at the age of thirty, God finally turned his situation around. Through a series of circumstances orchestrated by God, Joseph was raised to a very prominent position in the Egyptian government. But notice especially how his mind was healed and completely transformed even after years of being wounded by others:

> Now before the year of famine came, two sons were born to Joseph, whom Asenath, the daughter of Potiphera priest of On, bore to him. And Joseph named the first-born Manasseh, "For," he said, *"God has made me forget all my trouble and all my father's household."* And he named the second Ephraim, "For," he said, *"God has made me fruitful in the land of my affliction."* (Gen. 41:50–52, emphasis added)

God gave Joseph the ability not only to forget his affliction but to also rise above it and be fruitful in the very land where he had been afflicted. What a comfort to know that any painful memories we may have can be washed away by God and be replaced by His presence, power, and loving-kindness. You *can* get beyond the pain of yesterday and move forward to tomorrow. But you cannot do it on your own; only God can do it for you.

C. Determination. Paul knew he wasn't perfect, but he also realized that in the resurrection he would be. So he pressed on "toward the goal for the prize of the upward call of God in Christ Jesus" (Phil. 3:14). His focus was always on the future. He refused to allow himself to get snagged on his past. How did he do this? By *"forgetting* what lies behind and *reaching forward* to what lies ahead" (v. 13b, emphasis added). It is only as we leave the past behind that we can move ahead, pressing on toward new goals and the sin-free perfection that will one day be ours in Christ Jesus.

III. A Practical Response to Forgetting

Forgiving and forgetting—we often hear these paired with each other, yet painfully we realize that forgiving is usually much easier than forgetting. But the forgiving process is not complete until all offenses have been forgotten. As we grapple with this truth, three reminders will help us come to terms with it in our own lives.[1]

---

1. Outline points III.A.–C. may be found in the cassette message on forgetting, but they are not included in the book.

30

A. Forgetting reminds me that I, too, have flaws. If other people emphasized our flaws, we would not stand a chance. Realizing this will help us forget more easily the imperfections of others.

B. Forgetting enables me to be understanding and encouraging, not petty and negative. By disregarding the faults of others, we can find our way beyond a judgmental spirit and toward an attitude of encouragement.

C. Forgetting frees me to live for tomorrow rather than letting me be hung up on yesterday. We cannot press on toward tomorrow as God desires if we're dragging the weight of yesterday along with us.

IV. A Challenge: Two Questions

In looking at our lives as servants of Christ, two questions should periodically be asked to keep us on the right track.[2]

A. "Is there some offense I have refused to forget which keeps me from being happy and productive?" If so, declare it openly to the Lord and ask Him to take away the pain and the bitterness.

B. "Am I a victim of self-pity, living out my days emotionally paralyzed by anguish and despair?" If your answer is yes, then consider the consequences of living your life this way. Contrast this with the relief and joy of turning your misery over to the only One who can remove it—the Lord. He will enable you to make a fresh start.

 Living Insights

Study One ▬▬▬▬▬▬▬▬▬▬▬▬▬▬▬▬▬

Philippians 3:7–14 is a text of *action*. The Apostle Paul, like any good writer, emphasizes action through his usage of *verbs*. No dull, drab, lifeless phrasing here—it is powerful!

• Read through the text and circle all the verbs found in these eight verses. Then make a copy of this chart in your notebook. Jot down the verbs in the left column. With the help of a concordance, dictionary, and Bible dictionary, *define* each word. Finally, write in a brief statement about the verb's *significance* in the passage.

Continued on next page

---

2. Outline points IV.A.–B. are in the book, but they are not included on the cassette tape.

Active Forgetting—Philippians 3:7–14			
Verbs	Verses	Definitions	Significance

 Living Insights

Study Two ━━━━━━━━━━━━━━━━━━━━━━━━━━━━━━━━━━

Are you prepared to apply forgetting? It's probably one of the toughest assignments in our series, but it is necessary. Read over these suggestions and try to put them into practice.

- Meet with a close friend or family member and discuss your vulnerability. Do you come across as though you've "arrived"? Are you teachable? Do you freely admit when you're wrong? Are you the expert, above having needs? Communication like this will help you better understand how others perceive you.

- Paul refused to dwell on the past. How about you? Have you been hurt or mistreated by someone earlier in your life? What has been your response? Think through the biblical illustration of Joseph in Genesis 41. Are you willing to make the hard choice he did—forgive, forget, and go on—in spite of the pain? Carefully consider this.

- There's a logical progression of desirable qualities here. Honest vulnerability (meaning, I'm still learning) leads to authentic humility (I forget what's behind) which promotes the idea of moving ahead (I'm not quitting). As you can see, forgetting frees you from your past and opens up new vistas for your future. Since there are always new areas to seize and conquer, jot down on paper some specific things you would like to do to "press on." Use these as objectives to guide you in your new pursuits.

Thinking like a Servant Thinks

Romans 12, 2 Corinthians 10

Christians have always run the risk of being molded by the non-Christian philosophies that permeate their day. This is no less true in our era. Atheistic humanism and eastern pantheism bombard our minds from numerous fronts. These and other less prominent views threaten to alter our thinking and behavior to such a degree that our Christian faith could become anemic at best and nullified at worst. We who are Christ's servants need to beware of the enemies of our minds. We must alert ourselves to the perils which surround us and the devastation they can work within us if we drop our guard. We shall move toward this goal by discovering what the Bible teaches about servanthood thinking and what opposes it.

I. A "Renewed Mind" Is Essential (Romans 12:1–2)

In this portion of Scripture, the Apostle Paul tells us that we must have a renewed mind in order to think properly as Christians. Let's look at what he has to say.

> I urge you therefore, brethren, by the mercies of God, to present your bodies a living and holy sacrifice, acceptable to God, which is your spiritual service of worship. And do not be conformed to this world, but be transformed by the renewing of your mind, that you may prove what the will of God is, that which is good and acceptable and perfect.

Paul pleads with the believers in Rome to first present themselves to God as living sacrifices, then second to be transformed through the renewing of their minds. Paul knew that they had to break free from the world's anti-Christian thought forms, operational methods, styles, and techniques. He also understood that such a radical break could only occur as a result of a radical transformation that flows from within. In other words, in order to live differently, they had to begin thinking differently. *Right thinking precedes right actions.* A life characterized by serving others begins in a mind that is convinced that such a life is worth living. This explains why Paul, in another letter, exhorted believers toward authentic servanthood by appealing to them to model their minds after the mind of Christ, who was the greatest Servant of all (Phil. 2:5). We need to heed Paul's admonition in our own lives if we want to have the mind of Christ and thus think as a servant thinks.

II. Natural Thinking in Today's World (2 Corinthians 10:1–7)

The first step toward renewing our minds is to understand the characteristics of the unrenewed or natural mind. Our ability to identify them will aid us in ridding ourselves of these destructive

33

traits. In this section of Paul's letter to the Corinthian Christians, we can see five characteristics of the natural mind that were evident among some of the believers. As we consider these traits, honestly evaluate your own thinking and see if any of them apply to you.

A. Prejudice rather than objectivity (v. 2). Paul said that some in the Corinthian church regarded him and his companions as flesh-centered rather than Spirit-centered. They were prejudiced against Paul, his teaching, and his approach to life. So they assaulted his character and credentials (cf. 10:10–11, 11:12–15, 21–23) with the hope of discrediting him. A renewed mind doesn't think like this.

B. Focusing on the visible rather than the invisible (v. 3). Paul informs us that although he was mortal, he did not "war according to the flesh." That is, he refused to fight as the world does—with weapons of learning, personal influence, impressive credentials, rhetorical polish, and the like (cf. 1 Cor. 1:26, 2:1). Such a focus on externals could never lead to a truly transformed life. Yet that is where the world's sights are set—on the externals, not the internals.

C. Reliance on human strength rather than divine power (v. 4). This is the third characteristic of the natural mind. The world's mentality is to solve its problems and beat down its enemies with human power alone. Christians succumb to this way of thinking when they try to live day by day on the strength of their own resources instead of daily asking God to enable them through His all-sufficient power. But Paul says this is wrong! Why? Because "the weapons of our warfare are not of the flesh, but divinely powerful for the destruction of fortresses." Without God's strength working through us, we cannot win the spiritual warfare in which we are engaged.

D. Listening to people rather than to God (v. 5). Because people are in rebellion against God, it's only natural for them to oppose Him in any way they can. And since we who are Christians still sin, we can also oppose the Lord in numerous ways. This usually occurs when we ignore His instruction or substitute the contrary counsel of others for what is right.

E. Perceiving things superficially rather than deeply (v. 7). Paul stated it this way: "You are looking at things as they are *outwardly*. If anyone is confident in himself that he is Christ's, let him consider this again *within himself,* that just as he is Christ's, so also are we" (emphasis added). It is natural to judge things on the basis of appearances. But it doesn't take long to realize that appearances are often deceiving. Many times the truth can only be found by digging deep beneath the superficial.

III. Mental Barriers to God's Voice (2 Corinthians 10:4–5)

Paul lists four mental obstacles that obstruct, even block out, God's directives and counsel to us. The imagery he uses in communicating these barriers requires a bit of historical background for explanation's sake. In speaking about our minds, Paul depicts a fortified city. During his day huge walls were often built around cities for protection from enemy attack. Guards were posted on these walls to provide a constant watch and a means of further defense. Within the cities, towers were built high enough so that military officers and strategists could see over the walls for the purpose of directing their troops more effectively in the heat of battle. With this background in mind, let's look at Paul's various analogies to the mental barriers that guard our minds from God.

A. Analogy one: The wall, our mental "fortress." The fortress that God must destroy to get through to us is the wall that protects our natural mind-set. It may be built by prejudice, limited thinking, a negative spirit, or some other sinful material, but regardless, God cannot renew our minds without penetrating this destructive fortress.

B. Analogy two: The guards, our mental "speculations." These mental guards are the defense mechanisms, rationalizations, and other thinking patterns we employ to defend ourselves from the persistent advances of God's truth. In Romans 2:15 the word translated *thoughts* is the same Greek word as the one used here for *speculations.* And in the Romans passage, the guards of speculation mentioned are blame and justification. So we can see that when the Spirit of God moves against our mental fortresses, we often resist Him and defend our old thought patterns and behavior. Our natural minds do not want to be changed; they guard against it.

C. Analogy three: The towers, our mental "lofty things." This image carries the idea of something being lifted up or exalted. Of course, anything that we attempt to exalt "against the knowledge of God" (2 Cor. 10:5) has pride as its motive. Thus, for God to renew our minds, He must conquer our pride.

D. Analogy four: The strategists, our mental "thoughts." Accompanying our walls of resistance, our rationalizations that guard them, and our pride-motivated reactions that attempt to overtake God's truth are the actual thoughts and techniques we employ in our drive to ward off His Word and His prompting. These would include the thoughts we have that are alien to a renewed mind. God desires to capture and transform them so that they will fall in line with a thoroughly Christian mind-set.

IV. Supernatural Ability of the "Renewed Mind" (2 Corinthians 10:2–5, 11–12)

As the Lord tears down our mental barriers, He begins to renew our minds to be like Christ's mind. This brings us numerous benefits, four of which Paul mentions here. Let's look at each of them in the order in which they are given.

A. Courage against opposition (vv. 2–3). Paul said that he was courageous when faced by those who falsely regarded him as living his life in accord with fleshly principles rather than spiritual ones. A person with a renewed mind can stand firm against false accusations, misunderstandings, and other forms of mistreatment. He need not fear opposition no matter where it originates or what form it takes.

B. Divine power (v. 4). Servants with renewed minds are divinely empowered to destroy mental barriers and live authentic Christian lives.

C. Obedience to Christ (v. 5). A mind in the process of being fully transformed is gradually becoming more Christlike. And the more thoroughly Christ-centered it becomes, the easier it is for a servant to think and act from a Christian perspective.

D. Authentic independence (vv. 11–12). When we allow God to invade our fortified minds, He begins to replace hypocrisy with honesty and consistent obedience. He also exchanges the slavery of competition and comparison for the freedom of cooperation and an independent identity.

V. Servanthood Starts in the Mind

Our behavior and motives will never become Christlike until our minds begin the process of renewal. This means that authentic servanthood starts when mental transformation begins . . . and not until! So how can we begin the mind-renewal process and see it to its completion? There are two essential steps.

A. Operating from a renewed mind begins with a decision. You must decide that you want God to change your mind—to invade your fortress and destroy its barriers. It can all begin with a simple prayer: "Change me, Lord."

B. Continuing to operate from a renewed mind is a daily issue. Going through the transformation process is exactly that—a *process*. Our minds do not easily surrender to the invasion of God. Indeed, the war will only be won through our personal struggles in many daily battles. But take heart! God has promised us that the total victory is ours in Christ. This doesn't remove our struggles, but it gives us the hope and power we need to continue the fight.

Living Insights

J. B. Phillips said it well in his paraphrase of Romans 12:2: "Don't let the world around you squeeze you into its own mould."[1] In order to prevent the "squeeze" from being successful, we must renew our thinking.

- Using a copy of the following chart, write down some of the ways the world's prejudices affect your thinking. The influence of atheistic humanism and other non-Christian views is strong, isn't it? Next to these thoughts, record how God would have you think from a renewed mind. Jot down a Scripture verse or two that would support God's view. Study the contrasts . . . it should be revealing.

Thinking like a Servant Thinks		
The World's Prejudices	The Lord's Perspective	Scriptures

 Living Insights

This study clearly presented the issues in the quest for a renewed mind. There will be "fortresses," "speculations," "lofty things," and "thoughts" contrary to God, but victory is ours with God's power! Let's make this personal.

- Come to terms with where you are in your thinking. Are you checking your thoughts against God's thoughts? Is your thinking based on the Old and New Testaments? Do you see life as you wish it to be or as God has designed it to be?
- Often we forget that "renewing your mind" is a daily issue . . . moment by moment. This explains why our thinking often goes off course. Develop a game plan to keep "renewing your mind" uppermost in your thoughts. Then do your best to actively apply it in the moment-by-moment way God intended you to.

---

1. J. B. Phillips, *The New Testament in Modern English,* rev. ed. (New York: The Macmillan Co., 1972), p. 332.

Portrait of a Servant
(Part One)
Matthew 5

No series on servanthood would be complete without attention being paid to the Beatitudes, the opening words of Jesus' famous Sermon on the Mount. Unfortunately, the truth these words convey is usually foreign to our experience, though familiar to our ears. How little we exemplify character traits like gentleness, mercy, purity, and peacemaking. Yet an authentic servant should portray these qualities and more! In this study, let's commit ourselves to allowing the Holy Spirit to *conform* us into the image of Jesus Christ—the One who manifested the Beatitudes most consistently in His own life.

I. Jesus' Command: "Be Different!"

Throughout the Sermon on the Mount, Jesus exhorted His listeners to be different. Several times He couched His instruction in the words, " 'You have heard ... but I say to you ...' " (Matt. 5:21–22, 27–28, 33–34, 38–39, 43–44). In the middle of His sermon, He explained how His audience was to be different when praying, fasting, and giving to the needy (Matt. 6:2, 5, 16). In fact, the verse that probably best characterizes His teaching here begins, " 'Therefore, do not be like them' " (6:8). These observations make it obvious that Jesus wanted His followers to be different. But different from whom? In this sermon He called for His disciples to live contrasting lives to those of the hypocritical scribes and Pharisees, and the ungodly Gentiles (5:20, 47; 6:5, 7, 16, 32). Even after He finished speaking, His audience contrasted His authoritative instruction with the unauthoritative teaching of the scribes (7:28–29). In short, Jesus commanded that His disciples be humble and authentic instead of prideful and hypocritical. He called for a Christian counterculture—one that displayed a lifestyle which was at variance with that of the world's system. The Beatitudes form the heart of Jesus' command to be different.

II. The Beatitudes: Three Observations

We will examine the first four beatitudes in this lesson and the next four in the ensuing study. But before we begin to delve into each, let's step back for a moment and make some important overall observations of the eight servant qualities we find here.

A. Each identifies true servanthood. A Christian cannot choose to model a few of them and ignore the rest. All eight present necessary qualities that shape a servant's identity as well as his responsibility.

B. Each opens the door to inner happiness. The word *blessed* appears at the beginning of each beatitude in verses

3–10.[1] This term means "happy, fortunate." It's another way of saying, "Oh, how very happy are those who traffic in this truth." These eight traits, then, pave the way to deep satisfaction and contentment. It stands to reason that our failure to appropriate these qualities, in whole or in part, will cause us to fall short of the abiding joy we would otherwise experience.

C. Each has a corresponding promise. Notice that each beatitude has the same structure: "Blessed are they . . . for they shall . . ." The application of each trait to our lives will effect an accompanying promise which God will faithfully fulfill.

III. An Analysis of Four Beatitudes

The character traits we will deal with here are mentioned in Matthew 5:3–6. Remember, as we work through this portrait of servanthood, we need to recall that Jesus gave it for us to apply, not just appreciate.

A. "The poor in spirit" (v. 3). The section begins, " 'Blessed are the poor in spirit.' " Jesus did *not* say that those who were poor financially, without influence or prestige, or those oppressed by other people were blessed. These very common interpretations actually misconstrue His meaning. Jesus had in mind those who are spiritually bankrupt, who have nothing in themselves to give to God but their wholehearted trust in His grace. Jesus' words strike out at our pride—the attitude which falsely decrees that we are self-sufficient and thoroughly capable of controlling our own lives. In reality, our pride thinly veils our numerous inadequacies and leads us down a path that takes us further away from the only true Source of happiness—the living God. On the other hand, when we recognize our spiritual poverty and turn to Him in faith, Christ promises that ours will be the " 'kingdom of heaven.' " Those of us who depend totally on God to fill our spiritual void have His unalterable promise: We will have a place in Christ's everlasting kingdom (cf. Matt. 25:31–40, Rev. 21–22).

B. "Those who mourn" (v. 4). The Greek term translated *mourn* in this verse is the strongest one that could have been chosen. It was often used to describe a passionate lament for one who was greatly loved and suddenly lost. The word conveys the deep sorrow of a broken heart, mental anguish, and a penetrating ache in the soul. An individual's grieving over a personal loss, wrong in the world, the death of someone close, or even one's own sinfulness can all be clustered under this term. Furthermore, the word also includes *compassion*—a sincere caring for

---

1. Although verse 11 begins with *blessed,* it's not considered a separate beatitude; rather, it restates and amplifies verse 10.

others. Taking all this into account, perhaps a satisfactory paraphrase of this beatitude would be: "How happy are those who care intensely for the hurts, sorrows, and losses of others." Servants who manifest this trait, promises Christ, " 'shall be comforted.' " *Who* will be the channel or source of this returned comfort is not indicated. Perhaps it will come from the very individual who was comforted by an authentic servant. But regardless of whom it comes from, our Lord says that when we sincerely comfort others, comfort *will* be returned to us.

C. "The gentle" (v. 5). Many interpret this to say, "Blessed are the gentle, that is, those who are weak and spineless, for they shall be walked on by others." Although this is *not* what Jesus said, many have misunderstood Him to mean exactly that. A correct understanding of the Greek word translated *gentle* dispels this faulty interpretation. The original term is very rich and colorful. It conveys such qualities as strength under control, calmness in the midst of a pressurized atmosphere, soothing those who are angry or beside themselves, and a gracious courtesy that helps others to retain their self-esteem and dignity. The perfect Model of gentleness was Jesus Christ. He even described Himself as a gentle Person (Matt. 11:29). "But," someone may say, "it always seems that the strong and overpowering win. They seem to continually grow richer and more powerful at the expense of everyone else." From many outward appearances, this observation seems justified. However, God declares that this situation will not continue forever. Instead, He promises that the *gentle,* not the wickedly powerful, will ultimately " 'inherit the earth.' " In the end, the gentle will be the gainers, not the losers (cf. Ps. 37:7–11).

An Explanatory Note

The phrase "inherit the earth" may refer to the gentle who inherit parts of the earth in the present or receive all of the earth in the future. Perhaps the best way to understand the phrase is to take it as including both interpretations. For Scripture does record instances when His people displaced unbelievers and inherited their land (e.g., the Israelite takeover of Canaan under God's direction; see the Book of Joshua). The Bible also predicts a future period when saved Jews will inherit all the land God promised them (Jer. 3:18; cf. 33:14–16, Hosea 1:10–11) and when saved non-Jews (or Gentiles) will partake of the same inheritance yet be in a subservient role to the Jews (Isa. 14:1–2, 49:22–23, 61:5–9). This is called the Millennium, the period when Christ will reign over the earth for one thousand years (Rev. 20:4–6). Yet future to the Millennium, Scripture reveals God's creation of a new heaven and a new earth which all of His people, "the gentle" ones, will have as their inheritance forever. On the other hand, those who rejected Christ will be excluded from the earth and cast into hell forever (Rev. 20:11–15, 21:7–8).

D. **"Those who hunger and thirst for righteousness"** (v. 6). This is the fourth essential trait of a Christian servant. It's an insatiable appetite for what is right, a passionate drive for justice. And one is on the road to knowing what is right and just when one knows the Source and Basis of righteousness and justice—namely, the God of Scripture and creation. Thus, an eager, relentless pursuit of God permeates the life of the servant who hungers and thirsts for righteousness. Now there is also another side to this striving for a godly holiness, and that is an unwillingness to accept corruption, injustice, dishonesty, indeed *all* manifestations of moral compromise. The true servant of Christ not only desires but *works* toward the establishment of right on earth. He or she doesn't shrug off the lack of justice and purity as inevitable or allow it to continue without opposition. While servants pursue God in their own lives, they also fight ungodliness wherever they find it. In doing each, our Lord promises that " 'they shall be satisfied,' " both partially in the present and fully in the future. The Greek word for "satisfied" was commonly used in reference to the feeding and fattening of cattle. In other words, the insatiable appetite servants possess for holiness will be abundantly met. Our quest for godliness will lead to the contentment that only God can bring.

IV. Preliminary Questions to Answer
Although there are four more beatitudes left to cover, the ones we studied here have given us much to ponder. But just so we move beyond meditation and on toward application, let's pose several questions to ourselves and use the answers to direct our personal appropriation. Remember, be honest! Christian growth cannot begin or continue without honesty.

A. **"Am I really different?** Can my family, neighbors, and co-workers clearly tell that I am a Christian servant?"

B. **"Do I care if I'm not different?** Do I take Christ's words seriously enough to want to change?"

C. **"Do I really believe that serving others is one of the most Christlike attitudes I could have?"**

D. **"Will my knowledge of these character traits make any difference in my life *today?*"**

Living Insights

The Beatitudes are attainable character traits that mark the authentic servant of God. Since every quality is special in itself, let's analyze each one carefully.

● Make a copy of the following chart. Then conduct a scriptural search for each of these eight qualities. To make this easier, have a concordance handy; it can point you to other portions of God's Word that mention these traits. After you check the Scriptures, summarize your thoughts in the right column. Concentrate on the first four qualities now. The last four will be covered in the next lesson.

The Beatitudes: Portrait of a Servant		
Character Traits	Cross-references	Comments
Poor in Spirit (v. 3)		
Mournful (v. 4)		
Gentle (v. 5)		
Hungry and Thirsty for Righteousness (v. 6)		
Merciful (v. 7)		
Pure in Heart (v. 8)		
Peacemaker (v. 9)		
Persecuted (v. 10)		

 Living Insights

Looking at the first four qualities of a servant, one can't help but ask the question, How do I measure up to these traits? Let's see.

- Rate yourself on these characteristics by using the following scale: five is the best; one is the worst. Be honest.

		Poor in Spirit		
1	2	3	4	5

		Mournful		
1	2	3	4	5

		Gentle		
1	2	3	4	5

		Hungry and Thirsty for Righteousness		
1	2	3	4	5

- Write down one or two ways you can demonstrate these traits in the next week. Make your plans practical and fairly easy to manage. Then go for it!

Character Traits	Action Plans
Poor in Spirit	
Mournful	
Gentle	
Hungry and Thirsty for Righteousness	

Portrait of a Servant
(Part Two)
Matthew 5

Have you ever been to an art gallery? If you have, then you know how easy it is to become enthralled with a particularly good painting. You may first be attracted to its beauty or creative style. Then as you gaze at it more closely, you may find yourself studying its texture, mixture of colors, and shadings. The more extensively you examine it, the more you'll come to appreciate the artist's work and grant it higher value. In our last lesson we began to study one of the priceless portraits of a servant which is hanging in our Lord's multifaceted gallery—namely, the Beatitudes. Here we will return for a close look at the rest of the portrait. Our aim is to grasp the painting in its fullness so that we may become living portraits of the servant portrayed by the divine Artist.

I. Analysis of Four More Qualities

We already examined the first four servant traits Jesus gives in Matthew 5. In this lesson we'll walk our way through the last four qualities He mentions. Remember, our goal is not simply to gain more knowledge but to practice in daily life what we learn.

A. "The merciful" (v. 7). The passage reads, " 'Blessed are the merciful, for they shall receive mercy.' " Mercy is compassion for people in need; it's *active* concern for those who are hurting and suffering. The person who exercises mercy identifies with the one who is in pain. He or she doesn't simply pity the other person in his plight but gets into that person's skin—sees what he sees and feels what he feels. Consequently, the truly merciful are those who become personally involved and offer assistance that effectively eases some of the pain. Disinterest, detachment, and a lack of personal involvement are all contrary to the quality of mercy. It is no surprise, therefore, that when we peruse the pages of Scripture, the person we find exhibiting mercy most thoroughly is Jesus Christ. As the eternal Son of God, He chose to identify with us by taking on a human nature. By doing this, He personally experienced human hurts, temptations, pains, and sufferings, yet without committing a single sin. He entered our world of rebellion and strife and became like us so that He could provide a way to alleviate all our pain and hurt. And this He accomplished by dying in our place on the cross. Given these wonderful truths, it's little wonder that the writer of Hebrews penned these comforting words:

> Since then we have a great high priest who has passed through the heavens, Jesus the Son of God, let us hold fast our confession. For we do not have

a high priest who cannot sympathize with our weaknesses, but one who has been tempted in all things as we are, yet without sin. Let us therefore draw near with confidence to the throne of grace, *that we may receive mercy and may find grace to help in time of need.* (Heb. 4:14–16, emphasis added)

If we are to be His servants, then we need to concretely manifest the mercy He modeled for us. And when we do, He promises that we " 'shall receive mercy' " (Matt. 5:7b). Have you ever noticed that when needy people are significantly helped, they will usually return that kindness when their rescuers find themselves in difficult straits? This should come as no surprise, since Jesus promised that the merciful will have mercy returned to them.

B. **"The pure in heart"** (v. 8). The sixth characteristic of a servant is purity of heart. Like the first quality, poorness of spirit, this one emphasizes our inner man, our private world within. Jesus is saying that those who are *internally* clean are genuinely happy. They not only do the right things, they do them for the right reasons. They are free from hypocrisy and duplicity. Their private world is in order; they are inwardly holy, honest, and sincere. Jesus contrasted this trait with the impurity He found in the Pharisees. Though on the outside they appeared to be righteous and holy, on the inside they were corrupt and impure. They had the appearance of godliness, but in reality, they were phonies to the core. We can draw a strong contrast between the eight Beatitudes and Matthew 23, where Jesus pronounced eight "woes" to the Pharisees (vv. 13, 14, 15, 16, 23, 25, 27, 29). These judgments from Jesus reveal the true hearts of these Pharisees: they were concerned about maintaining an outward godly appearance but unconcerned about developing a true inner godliness. The elements that comprise purity of heart were virtually absent from the lives of these religious leaders. Unfortunately, many Christians today live the life of a first-century Pharisee. Of course, they have updated the list of externals to be religiously obeyed, but their internal phoniness remains unaltered.

A Personal Application

Are you a modern-day Pharisee? Do you find yourself focusing on the externals rather than the internals, your public life rather than your private life? If so, don't try to justify your condition; that will only lead you further down the road of hypocrisy. Also, don't despair over your internal impurity. God is in the business of cleaning up

---

lives. He can purify yours if you really want Him to. All you need to do is confess your sin to Him and ask Him to cleanse you. Then trust Him to honor your request (for He certainly will), and, in the power of His Holy Spirit, daily seek to do His written will. A study in Romans 6–8 will help you considerably in this endeavor.

C. **"The peacemakers"** (v. 9). Matthew 5:9 is the only place in the New Testament where the Greek term translated *peacemakers* is used. And a clear understanding of its meaning is essential for grasping the thrust of Jesus' instruction here. So let's achieve this goal by first noting what *peacemaker* does not mean, then examining what it does mean. This word does *not* refer to people who avoid all conflict, those who are relaxed and easygoing, people who compromise their convictions to appease those who disagree, or even individuals who work for peace at any price. Instead, peacemakers are servants who are *internally at ease with themselves* and thus are not abrasive. As a result, they are not passive; they work diligently to settle quarrels rather than advance or even start them. Briefly put, peacemakers are those who pursue both internal and external peace as far as they can. Paul states the idea in this way: "If possible, so far as it depends on you, be at peace with all men" (Rom. 12:18). Later, he reinforces his words with this admonition: "So then let us pursue the things which make for peace and the building up of one another" (14:19). As we consider these things, we can see that the opposite of peacemaking is troublemaking. James clearly contrasts these two conditions when he says,

> For where jealousy and selfish ambition exist, there is disorder and every evil thing. But the wisdom from above is first pure, then peaceable, gentle, reasonable, full of mercy and good fruits, unwavering, without hypocrisy. And the seed whose fruit is righteousness is sown in peace by those who make peace. (James 3:16–18)

No wonder Jesus says that peacemakers, not troublemakers, are the happy and satisfied ones! He also adds that peacemakers " 'shall be called sons of God' " (Matt. 5:9b). In other words, people will see in them a quality that is godlike. Hence, peacemakers will stand out from the crowd as representatives of God.

D. **"Those who have been persecuted"** (v. 10). At first glance, it seems odd that a beatitude on persecution would immediately follow one on peacemakers. Realistically, however, those who do what is right are often wronged. After all, we live in a world where right is commonly belittled and wrong is encouraged, even exalted. Therefore, those of us who are peacemakers should expect to be persecuted and abused. Indeed, Jesus goes on to say, " 'Blessed are you *when* men cast insults at you, and persecute you, and say all kinds of evil against you falsely, on account of Me' " (v. 11, emphasis added). He knows that vicious ill-treatment is more than a mere possibility in a Christian's life; it is highly probable that persecution will occur. But believers should not grow bitter or become downcast when they experience troubled times because of their faith. Rather, says Christ, they should rejoice and be glad. Why? Because their heavenly reward—their inheritance of the kingdom of heaven—will be great (vv. 10, 12). So when we suffer verbal, psychological, or physical abuse at the hands of others because of our stand for Christ and what is right, we should count it all joy, for it will only increase our ultimate rewards in heaven. Notice also that believers have been persecuted for many centuries, even before Jesus' day (v. 12b). In fact, take a moment to read Hebrews 11:35–38. There you will find a brief but descriptive account of how severely many of God's people were abused, maligned, tortured... even put to death during ancient times, not to mention the centuries following the Resurrection of Christ. We need not feel alone when we experience the brunt of mistreatment, for countless others have preceded us and many more will follow.

II. A Last Look at the Portrait

What would you say if Jesus were to ask you, "What would you like to be when you grow up?" After looking at the portrait He gives in the Beatitudes, there's no question how He would want you to answer: "Jesus, I want to be a servant." "Then," He would say, "you must be poor in spirit, compassionate, gentle, a pursuer of righteousness, merciful, pure in heart, a peacemaker, and a joyful endurer of persecution. These qualities are impossible for you to attain on your own. But if you give your life to Me in faith and use the power of My Spirit to obey My counsel, then you will become a living portrait of a Christian servant. The price you'll pay will be great; however, the rewards you'll receive will be greater still. Come with Me and we'll get started."

Living Insights

Study One ▰▰▰▰▰▰▰▰▰▰▰▰▰▰▰▰▰▰▰▰▰▰▰▰▰▰▰

Let's continue our scriptural search for the qualities mentioned in the Beatitudes. Remember, this is a passage presenting the style of a real servant. Your study will be time well spent.

- Return to the chart you constructed in "Portrait of a Servant" (Part One). In that lesson we looked at the first four qualities of servanthood. Let's look at the last four, beginning with *merciful* in verse 7. Review the instructions in that study and complete the chart.

 Living Insights

Study Two ▰▰▰▰▰▰▰▰▰▰▰▰▰▰▰▰▰▰▰▰▰▰▰▰▰▰▰

An increase in spiritual maturity involves the development of a more Christlike character. Perhaps we could summarize this desirable process with one probing question: As you grow older in the Lord, is your life looking more like the portrait of a servant?

- Unhurriedly read over the personal questions given in Living Insights, study two (found at the end of the previous lesson). They all lead to action, don't they? Discover some ways you can put a real difference and a genuine concern into your lifestyle throughout the next few days. Follow through with your plan and check back in a few days to see if it's working!

The Influence of a Servant

2 Timothy 3, Matthew 5

How can servants impact a tough, hard world? What possible influence could the people described in the Beatitudes exert in a society overrun with competitive, stubborn, aggressive, often hostile individuals? What lasting good can the gentle, the pure, the peacemakers, the persecuted, and the merciful bring to the world? Wouldn't they become trampled underfoot and overwhelmed by the flood tide of wickedness? Aren't such people too feeble to achieve anything, especially since they are such a small remnant? As we shall discover, Jesus did not share this skepticism. Rather, He emphasized the *reverse*. He declared that His servants were sources of indispensable ingredients that preserve and illumine a planet filled with corruption and darkness.

I. A Critical Estimation of Our Times (2 Timothy 3)

We need not look far or hard for an accurate analysis of the world in which we live. All we have to do is turn in the Bible to 2 Timothy 3. There we find that Paul's assessment of his first-century world fits our times as well. We could summarize what he says in three words.

A. "Difficult" (v. 1). We're told that *"difficult* times will come" (emphasis added). Some scholars have translated this term as *terrible* or *perilous*. The Greek root word from which this term comes means "grievous, harsh, fierce, savage." It's used only one other time in the New Testament—Matthew 8:28. There we read of two demon-possessed men whose consequent behavior was "exceedingly violent." That's an excellent description of our world—violent, harsh, perilous, difficult.

B. "Depraved" (v. 8). Here Paul cites two men from Moses' day as prime examples of man's ungodly state apart from salvation. Paul describes them as being of a "depraved mind"—that is, as possessing a corrupted or ruined understanding of the truth. A world filled with people such as these is indeed a difficult place in which to live.

> **A Theological Clarification**
>
> Throughout church history, Christians have believed in the depravity of man, but they have voiced differences over the meaning and extent of depravity. Without entering into the details of this intramural debate, we can turn to God's authoritative Word and discern what it clearly teaches about man's sinful condition. By doing so, we will learn the parameters God has established for understanding the depravity of man. **First,** the Bible gives several models which depict human depravity. For example, man is dead in sin and needs new life (Eph. 2:1–6;

Col. 2:13); he's sick with sin and in need of healing (Mark 2:17); he's impoverished by sin and needs God's riches (Luke 4:18, 2 Cor. 8:9, Eph. 2:7); he's polluted or defiled by sin and needs to be cleansed (Mark 7:14–23, Eph. 5:25–27, Titus 1:15, 1 John 1:7–9); he's lost in the darkness of sin and desperately needs the light of Christ (John 8:12, 12:35); he's blinded by sin and needs his sight restored (Luke 4:18, 2 Cor. 4:3–6); and he's enslaved to sin and needs to be set free from it (Luke 4:18, John 8:31–36, Rom. 6:16–18). **Second,** the Scriptures declare that all human beings are depraved, not just some (Eccles. 7:20, 29; Rom. 3:9–18, 23). **Third,** because sin has affected every aspect of man, he is in need of being sanctified or purified entirely (1 Thess. 5:23). **Fourth,** depraved man can do some good things (Matt. 7:9–11), but there is no good work he can perform that could possibly save him (Isa. 64:6, Gal. 2:16, Eph. 2:8–9, Titus 3:3–7). **Fifth,** depravity does not mean that man is as bad as he could be, for the biblical description of the still-future Tribulation period shows that he has the potential to be even worse than he is now (Matt. 24:4–13; 2 Thess. 2:1–12; Rev. 9:18, 20–21, 16:8–11). **Sixth,** neither does depravity mean that man is evil *in himself,* for Scripture teaches that *everything* God created is still intrinsically good though effaced by sin (Mark 7:14–23; Rom. 8:18–23, 14:14; 1 Tim. 4:4; Titus 1:15). Given all this, *we can conclude that human depravity means that all human beings are morally and spiritually corrupt because of sin.* On their own, therefore, they are unwilling to seek out and accept God's gracious provision for salvation. Rather than bow before God with hands open to receive His free gift of life, people stand with clenched fists raised in open defiance against heaven. That's depravity! Thus, without God in His mercy persuasively moving throughout the world to draw all people freely to Himself, no one ever could be saved (Matt. 23:37; John 1:12–13, 6:44–45, 16:8–11; 1 Tim. 2:3–4; 1 Pet. 1:1–3; 2 Pet. 3:9).

C. **"Deceived"** (v. 13). The world around us is also teeming with imposters and deceivers—people who pretend to offer help but who actually oppose the truth and promote evil. Unfortunately, they flourish in every profession, providing false hope for true needs.

II. **Indispensable Influences for Our Good** (Matthew 5:13–16)

Technically, the only One who can preserve this world is Jesus Christ. But as His servants, we have been commissioned by Him to carry on this work in His absence. In one of His best-known and best-loved sermons, the Sermon on the Mount, Jesus addressed our task through His use of two metaphors—salt and light. Let's take time to reread these very familiar verses:

> "You are the salt of the earth; but if the salt has become tasteless, how will it be made salty again? It is good for nothing any more, except to be thrown out and trampled under foot by men. You are the light of the world. A city set on a hill cannot be hidden. Nor do men light a lamp, and put it under the peck-measure, but on the lampstand; and it gives light to all who are in the house. Let your light shine before men in such a way that they may see your good works, and glorify your Father who is in heaven."

A. **"The salt of the earth"** (v. 13). It's interesting to note that when Jesus described the qualities of a servant throughout the Beatitudes (vv. 3–12), He used the words *they, their,* and *those.* But when He spoke of the servant's influence upon society, He personalized His words by using the term *you.* In this way, He made His metaphor stronger and more direct. He said, " 'You are the salt of the earth.' " How can we be salt? To find out, let's consider the two distinct uses of salt. First, salt can be used as a preservative. In fact, years ago, before refrigeration, salt was used to keep meat from rotting and to preserve it in an edible condition. So if we are the preserving agents of the world, then it, too, must be perishing. But Christ emphasized that our influence keeps the corruption from coming to completion. Second, salt is also useful for taste; it enhances the flavor of numerous foods. But when salt loses its taste, it becomes " 'good for nothing any more, except to be thrown out and trampled under foot by men.' " In Jesus' day tasteless salt was mixed with other ingredients in order to fill holes in the roads. By analogy He is warning His servants that if they lose their preserving influence in society, they will become only as useful as the dirt which fills potholes. Before we move on, let's briefly observe three more facts about salt. First, *salt is shaken and sprinkled, not poured.* It has to be spread out; too much in one place will ruin the taste of the food. The same is true for Christians; they need to break out of their holy huddles and spread themselves throughout the playing field. Second, *salt adds flavor, but it's obscure*—it doesn't draw attention to itself but to the food it's

51

seasoning. Likewise, Christ's servants should add a zest and flavor to life that would be impossible to achieve without them. Third, *salt is unlike any other seasoning.* It cannot be duplicated, and it must be applied before it is useful. Similarly, non-Christians cannot be the salt of the earth—only Christians can. However, Christians cannot preserve and season society if they don't reach out beyond themselves.

   B. **"The light of the world"** (vv. 14–16). Elsewhere Jesus said of *Himself,* " 'I am the light of the world; he who follows Me shall not walk in the darkness, but shall have the light of life' " (John 8:12). In Matthew 5, however, Jesus said that *Christians* are the light of the world. In other words, when we become His servants, His light shines through us to a world in darkness. Light's basic function is to dispel darkness. But, as Jesus points out, light cannot perform its job if it is hidden. Therefore, He exhorts us to let our lights stand out, plain for all to see, not just for a select or comfortable few. But what are the lights of our lives? He answers that for us in verse 16: " 'Let your light shine before men in such a way that they may see your *good works* '" (emphasis added). As we think of light, let's take note of three characteristics. First, *light is silent.* It makes no noise, and it doesn't call attention to itself—it merely shines. And yet, in so doing, it offers a profound appeal to those who see it from the darkness. Second, *light gives direction.* It exposes what the dark has veiled and illumines the pathway through the many obstructions. Third, *light attracts attention.* Those in the dark cannot fail to see the light when it pierces through. As we live our lives in obedience to God, others will readily see the radical difference from their own lifestyles.

III. A Personal Response to Our Role

God calls us to be different from everyone else in the world. But this kind of revolutionary lifestyle requires a daily commitment that lasts a lifetime. To keep the salt good and the light burning brightly, we need to plan an active response, which begins with three realizations.

   A. **"I am different."** We who know Christ are unique. In no way should we conform to the ungodly system of this world.

   B. **"I am responsible."** We are each responsible for our own salt, that it keeps its preserving power, and our own light, that it continues to shine brightly for Christ.

   C. **"I am influential."** Christians who are salt and light are influential to those around them. The only question is, Will we as Christians influence non-Christians in a way that is pleasing or displeasing to our Lord? The choice and responsibility belong to us.

Living Insights

How can servants influence this godless world in which we live? Christ presents a positive approach in His Sermon on the Mount. A good starting point in this challenge is to learn a little more from God's perspective on *who the people are who make up the world's system.*

*   Copy this chart into your notebook. Now carefully read 2 Timothy 3:2–5. In these four verses you can find twenty characteristics of worldly people. Write each trait in the left column. Look for possible cross-references with other Scriptures and jot them down in the middle column. Then summarize your thoughts in the right column. When this is completed, go back and contrast this chart with the eight characteristics of a servant in "Portrait of a Servant." There's a big difference . . . wouldn't you agree?

Portrait of the World—2 Timothy 3:2–5		
Character Traits	Cross-references	Comments

 Living Insights

"I am different. I am responsible. I am influential." The task of being salt and light to the world is a crucial one indeed. Let's work together on some ways to increase our "bite" and "brightness"!

*   Gather your close Christian friends or family together and discuss your impact on the world. Are you different? Are you shining brightly? Would it be a surprise to a person in your office or neighborhood if someone pointed to you and said, "Did you know that that person is a Christian?" Talk about *positive* ways to underscore the differences!

*   The world's system is characterized by difficult times, depraved minds, and deceived people (2 Tim. 3:1–13). Read Romans 1:18–32.

Continued on next page

By spending some time in that passage, it should become increasingly clear that God wants us to be salt with bite and lights that shine in this dark, decaying world.

- You are influential. Do you really believe that? Do others see your life and glorify your Father? Perhaps you've never worked through this concept. Sit back and begin to write the names of five people you influence on a regular basis. Describe that influence in detail and rate it as poor, mediocre, or challenging. Close by asking God to cause your life to be a helpful influence to others for His glory.

The Perils of a Servant

2 Corinthians 4, 2 Kings 4–5

While there are occupational hazards in all callings, the perils related to servanthood are especially subtle. Although the servant is by no means immune to the temptations of the flesh, the dangers to be guarded against most lie in the realm of the spirit. With *relentless* determination, the enemy of our souls will take advantage of every inch of ground we concede in any area of our lives. Make no mistake about it, no servant—no matter how dedicated or how unselfish—is totally safe from the peculiar perils and traps of our adversary, Satan. To be forewarned is to be forearmed. Listen up, servants!

I. Some Common Misconceptions (2 Corinthians 4:7–13)

There are several mistaken ideas people have about servants of God. In 2 Corinthians 4, Paul mentions three of which we should be aware.

A. Servants have special powers in themselves (2 Cor. 3:5, 4:7).

How easy it is to look at God's most successful servants as though they were extrahuman. We often put them high on a pedestal, all the while forgetting about their humanity. Paul is quick to point out, though, that the power God's servants possess comes entirely from the Lord. Take note of his words:

> Not that we are adequate in ourselves to consider anything as coming from ourselves, but our adequacy is from God. (3:5)

> But we have this treasure in earthen vessels, that the surpassing greatness of the power may be of God and not from ourselves. (4:7)

Paul reminds us that servants are completely human and not bionic supersaints or minigods.

B. Servants don't struggle with everyday problems (4:8–9).

Notice the words Paul uses to describe the everyday life of a servant: *afflicted, perplexed, persecuted, struck down.* These words reflect the struggles of life that are common to all of us.[1]

C. Servants are protected against subtle dangers (4:10–13).

Paul said that we always carry "about in the body the dying of Jesus" (v. 10a). Paul lived his own Christian life in the jaws of death and was constantly under the subtle attack of the temptations to which no servant is immune (vv. 11–13; cf. 2 Cor. 1:8–10, 6:4–5, 11:23–33; Gal. 6:17; Heb. 11:32–40; James 1:2–4). God never promises His followers that they will travel a

---

1. For a closer look at the meanings of these words, see study fourteen, "The Consequences of Serving."

path without obstructions and pitfalls. Instead, He promises to enable them to endure their struggles (1 Cor. 10:13).

II. A Classic Example (2 Kings 4–5)

What Paul explains, we can see illustrated in the life of an obscure man named Gehazi, Elisha's servant. But before we consider what his experience can teach us, let's pause and gain some essential background data.

A. **Background and role.** Gehazi lived during the reign of the wicked king Jehoram (852–841 B.C.), ruler of the northern kingdom of Israel. These were difficult days in Israel's history. For three hundred years there had not been one king who had walked with God. The entire period had been marked by compromise, murder, gross immorality, and idolatry. In the midst of this evil came the prophet Elijah. And when his lifetime on earth drew to a close, another prophet named Elisha replaced him and carried on God's work among His wayward people (2 Kings 2). Without Elijah, however, Elisha was alone. And because he needed the assistance and support of a friend, God gave him Gehazi. As the story unfolds in 2 Kings 4, we can see that Gehazi's role was one of a servant to Elisha. The account records that a prominent woman who lived in Shunem perceived from Elisha's frequent visits that he was a " 'holy man of God' " (4:9). So she had her husband build a small room for him to occupy during his visits (v. 10). During one of his stays, Elisha requested that Gehazi call the Shunammite woman and ask her how they could return her generous hospitality. After speaking with her, Gehazi told Elisha that she was childless and implied that there was little hope for her situation to change since her husband was old. So Elisha had Gehazi call her again, whereupon the prophecy of Elisha was given, namely, that she would " 'embrace a son' " during the same season the following year (v. 16). And so it happened, just as Elisha had said (vv. 11–17).

B. **Temptations and reactions.** Gehazi's position alongside this prophet of God was privileged. Yet, as we shall discover, it was not without its temptations—the same ones God's servants still face today. The story picks up years later when the Shunammite woman's son is grown. He suddenly becomes sick and dies on his mother's lap. She recalls Elisha's role in bringing her son into her life and makes preparations to seek him out at Mount Carmel (4:18–24).

   1. **The peril of overprotection and possessiveness** (4:25–28). Servants of God are given certain ministries to perform and are often called to accomplish these tasks under the authority of others. This can breed within a

servant the tendency to possess and jealously guard the ministry in which he or she is involved. Gehazi fell into this very trap. When the Shunammite woman came to Elisha, fell down before him, and grabbed his feet, Gehazi "came near to push her away" (v. 27). His intentions were good; he was only trying to protect Elisha. But his action displayed his tunnel vision—a perspective which grows from the soil of overprotection and possessiveness. All he saw was a woman infringing upon his superior, not a mother who was deeply disturbed and seeking Elisha's help. In the Book of Numbers we discover a similar situation between Joshua and Moses. Joshua was concerned about two men prophesying in the Israelite camp. He felt that what they were doing was Moses' job and his alone. So he urged Moses to stop them. Moses refused. He even told Joshua that he would be pleased if " 'all the Lord's people were prophets' " (Num. 11:29a). Unlike Joshua, Moses had not succumbed to the temptation to keep an exclusive hold on the ministry God had given him. Just as Moses handled Joshua, so Elisha corrected Gehazi.

2. **The peril of feeling used and unappreciated** (4:29–41). After the woman informed Elisha of her son's death, he instructed Gehazi: " 'Gird up your loins and take my staff in your hand, and go your way; . . . and lay my staff on the lad's face' " (2 Kings 4:29). And Gehazi obeyed. He "laid the staff on the lad's face, but there was neither sound nor response" (v. 31a). Then Gehazi returned to Elisha and told him what had happened, so Elisha went himself and healed the boy (vv. 31–36). In another incident, Gehazi made a pot of stew to feed "the sons of the prophets" (v. 38b). But while it was cooking, someone added wild gourds, not knowing they were poisonous. As the men were eating the stew, they cried out, " 'O man of God, there is death in the pot' " (v. 40). So Elisha threw a handful of meal into the stew, which dispelled the poison (v. 41). Given events such as these, it isn't difficult to imagine what Gehazi must have felt. Discouragement, frustration, the sting of not being appreciated—all these feelings and more probably tormented him and began to break down his attitude toward Elisha. After all, Elisha received all the credit, while Gehazi's faithful service went unnoticed.

3. **The peril of disrespect and resentment** (5:1–19). As we move on in this story, we find Gehazi placed in a different situation. A high-ranking military officer known as Naaman came to Elisha's house for cleansing from leprosy. As

Naaman stood in the doorway of the house, Elisha sent his messenger (probably Gehazi) with this message: " 'Go and wash in the Jordan seven times, and your flesh shall be restored to you and you shall be clean' " (v. 10). Naaman was outraged! He stomped away and said, " 'Behold, I thought, "He will surely come out to me, and stand and call on the name of the Lord his God, and wave his hand over the place, and cure the leper" ' " (v. 11). Notice who took the brunt of Naaman's anger—Gehazi! He obediently delivered Elisha's message, but instead of receiving gratitude or praise, he was treated with disrespect and cutting resentment.

   4. **The peril of hidden greed** (5:13–27). Naaman's servants spoke to him and convinced him to follow Elisha's instructions. When he did, he experienced complete cleansing from the leprosy (vv. 13–14). Afterward, he went to Elisha and offered him a present, but Elisha refused to take it (vv. 15–16). Gehazi, however, let his greed seize the opportunity. Even though Naaman had already gone, Gehazi pursued him with the following request: " 'My master has sent me, saying, "Behold, just now two young men of the sons of the prophets have come to me from the hill country of Ephraim. Please give them a talent of silver and two changes of clothes" ' " (v. 22). Obviously, Gehazi lied to Naaman in order to get something for himself. But his sin didn't go unpunished. When he returned home, Elisha confronted him with a simple question: " 'Where have you been, Gehazi?' " Gehazi lied again; he said that he had not gone anywhere (v. 25). But Elisha knew better. He exposed Gehazi's greed, then afflicted him with Naaman's leprosy (vv. 26–27).

III. Some Lingering Lessons

There is a secret, smoldering desire in all of us to be rewarded and exalted. But if our hearts are truly with God and our focus is on Him, it will be easier for us to be patient and wait. He *will* abundantly reward our service, but in His own time. Until then, we should beware of the perils illustrated in Gehazi's life and recall to mind the following three truths:

   A. **No servant is completely safe.** The more you serve others, the harder you need to lean on the enabling Master. The perils of service *will* come, but the Lord will help you avoid them by enabling you to maintain a proper perspective.

   B. **Most deeds will be initially unrewarded.** More often than not, your service will be overlooked. But remember that your imperishable reward will not come from other people but

from God. He will give you the sense of deep satisfaction you
need to carry on and be fulfilled.

C. All motives must be honestly searched. You should
never jump into a task without asking yourself why you want to
do it. Keep an honest check on your motives. Self-examination
can only benefit you in the long haul.

 Living Insights

Study One ━━━━━━━━━━━━━━━━━━━━━━━━━━━━━━━━━━━

The story of Gehazi is one rich in application to servants of any time
in history. Let's return to this story and dig even deeper into the perils
of servanthood.

- Check out all the Scriptures from 2 Kings in the preceding outline.
  A good way to increase your understanding of this passage is to *ask
  questions.* Make a copy of the following chart. It should aid you in
  categorizing your questions and answers so that you will discover
  all that the text records about Gehazi.

The Perils of a Servant: Gehazi	
Questions	Answers
Who?	
What?	
Where?	
When?	
Why?	
How?	

 Living Insights

Study Two ━━━━━━━━━━━━━━━━━━━━━━━━━━━━━━━━━━━

Our study concluded with three lingering lessons. Let's use our Living
Insights to work through them. We don't want to be guilty of Gehazi's
responses; thus, we need to be prepared.

- No servant is safe from perils. Write down the ones that especially
  plague you. It could be that you have additional struggles not
  mentioned. Add these to your list. Conclude by writing next to each
  peril the *proper* perspective based on God's Word.

Continued on next page

- Take a long, hard look at your motives. Ask yourself, Why am I doing this? Why do I take this position? Why am I helping this person? *You* are the only one who is able to answer questions of motive.
- Are you in a significant position yet receiving no credit? Are you responsible for making others successful? Are you jealous of the "applause" they're receiving? If you are in any one of these positions, it would be beneficial for you to sit down and talk with the other person or persons involved. It could be your husband or wife, boss or secretary, foreman or crew member, or perhaps just a friend. Share your feelings and strive anew to work together.

The Obedience of a Servant

Matthew 11, John 13

No series on servanthood would be complete without attention given to the subject of obedience. After all, without obedience, a servant is *not* a servant. And therein lies the secret of greatness in one's character. As one man put it, "Every great person has first learned how to obey, whom to obey, and when to obey."[1] Jesus our Lord personified obedience. He openly declared that He accomplished the work the Father gave Him to do (John 17:4)—a task that was successful because He actively subjected His will to the will of the Father (John 4:34, 5:30, 6:38). Therefore, if we are to live as Christ lived, obedience must mark our lives.

I. Self-description of Jesus

The testimonies of men and women concerning Christ have abounded through many centuries, including our own. We have probably heard several ourselves. But how often have we stopped to examine what Jesus had to say about Himself? If we are to follow His example, then we should know how Jesus characterized His own life. With this in mind, let's look at His self-description:

> "Take My yoke upon you, and learn from Me, for *I am gentle and humble in heart;* and you shall find rest for your souls." (Matt. 11:29, emphasis added)

Jesus used two words to describe Himself. Let's look at each more closely.

A. "I am gentle." The Greek word rendered "gentle" is *praűs.* It speaks of strength under control. It's the same word that was often used to describe the taming of a wild horse or an ointment that takes the sting out of a wound. That's Christ—strong, yet very much under control.

B. "I am ... humble." *Tapeinós,* which means "to be made low," is the Greek term used for "humble." In our lives, where power and prestige are sought and exalted, it's quite unusual to hear a person unashamedly describe himself as humble. But that's what Jesus did, because that's what a servant is ... and His is the eminent Model of servanthood. Jesus' desire for us is that we become just like Him—not weak, spineless, or unusable, but strong, firm, and readily available to meet the needs of others.

II. Illustration of Jesus' Self-description

The beauty of Christ's example is that He demonstrated in His own life what He taught others to do. So by looking at His actions,

---

1. William A. Ward, *Quote Unquote,* compiled by Lloyd Cory (Wheaton: Victor Books, 1977), p. 222.

we can glean how He wants us to act as obedient servants. In John 13:3–17, we'll set our sights on an account familiar to many of us—Jesus' washing of the disciples' feet. *Warning:* Don't allow its familiarity to breed contempt for its message! In this text Jesus graphically illustrates that obedience and service are like Siamese twins—inseparable! Thus, we fail to serve when we disobey, and we cannot obey unless we humbly serve. Let's carefully examine this passage together.

A. Background information. In our society, washing the feet of another is unnecessary since it has lost the function it once had. But it was a very common practice in the days of Christ. The streets of that time were extremely dusty, and when it rained, they turned to mud. It's little wonder that feet covered only by open sandals became very dirty. Therefore, it was customary for a servant to greet arriving guests at the door and remove their dirty sandals and clean their feet. If the owner of a house could not afford a servant, one of the early-arriving guests would graciously assume this task for the others.

B. Personal demonstration. *Not one* of Jesus' disciples volunteered to do this job as they came together for the Passover meal. So Jesus took on the servant's role in order to teach His disciples what obedient servanthood was all about. Let's look at the account as it unfolds.

> Jesus, knowing that the Father had given all things into His hands, and that He had come forth from God, and was going back to God, rose from supper, and laid aside His garments; and taking a towel, girded Himself about. Then He poured water into the basin, and began to wash the disciples' feet, and to wipe them with the towel with which He was girded. And so He came to Simon Peter. He said to Him, "Lord, do You wash my feet?" Jesus answered and said to him, "What I do you do not realize now, but you shall understand hereafter." Peter said to Him, "Never shall You wash my feet!" Jesus answered him, "If I do not wash you, you have no part with Me." Simon Peter said to Him, "Lord, not my feet only, but also my hands and my head." Jesus said to him, "He who has bathed needs only to wash his feet, but is completely clean; and you are clean, but not all of you." For He knew the one who was betraying Him; for this reason He said, "Not all of you are clean." (vv. 3–11)

As we view Christ's actions in this situation, at least three observations stand out.

1. **Serving is unannounced.** Nowhere do we find Christ telling the disciples that He was about to demonstrate humble, obedient service. He simply rose from the meal, poured a basin of water, and began to wash their feet.
2. **Serving includes receiving graciously as well as giving graciously.** When Jesus approached Peter to wash his feet, Peter protested. He was obviously unwilling to make himself vulnerable—a reluctance that revealed his pride. This shows us that it takes humility on our part to allow another person to minister to us.
3. **Serving is not a sign of inner weakness but incredible strength.** Jesus rebuked Peter when He said to him, " 'If I do not wash you, you have no part with Me' " (v. 8b). Being a servant sometimes involves confrontation, as Jesus so clearly revealed. For us to do as He did requires great strength and loving courage.

C. **Direct admonition.** When Jesus finished washing their feet, He rejoined them at the table and asked a question: " 'Do you know what I have done to you?' " (v. 12). There was obviously more to His actions than the mere washing of feet. Notice how He answered His own question.

"You call Me Teacher and Lord; and you are right, for so I am. If I then, the Lord and the Teacher, washed your feet, you also ought to wash one another's feet. For I gave you an example that you also should do as I did to you. Truly, truly, I say to you, a slave is not greater than his master; neither is one who is sent greater than the one who sent him. If you know these things, you are blessed if you do them." (vv. 13–17)

Jesus first emphasized His authoritative position as Lord and Teacher. Then He followed His declaration with an unexpected twist: He commanded them not to wash *His* feet but to wash *each other's* feet. Washing the feet of the Savior would have been no problem—it would even have been expected. But to serve each other with such humility—that was a different story! The same is true today, isn't it?

III. **Appropriation of Christ's Admonition**
In John 13, we are left with the same command Christ gave to His disciples. It goes far beyond foot washing. Jesus saw a need, and He did something about it. There wasn't a long prayer or lengthy discussion period—He silently stooped down and did the job that needed to be done. He commands us to do the same, and that requires obedience. There are three observations from this account that we can make about obedience. Each will help us to personally appropriate His command.

A. Obedience means personal involvement (v. 14). We cannot meet needs from a distance. Like Jesus, we must reach beyond ourselves and touch the needy around us in practical, concrete ways.

B. Obedience requires Christlike unselfishness (v. 15). We cannot minister effectively if we are unwilling to take risks and give up things from our own lives. We must see people as Christ sees them. When we do, we'll realize that no personal sacrifice is too great in serving others.

C. Obedience results in ultimate happiness (v. 17). As Jesus said, " 'If you know these things, you are blessed if you do them.' " Knowledge should lead to obedient action, which will result in divine blessing. Our knowledge of the truth must precede our performance of it. But if we fail to do what we know we should, we will not experience the lasting happiness that only God can give.

 Living Insights

Study One ▬▬▬▬▬▬▬▬▬▬▬▬▬▬▬▬▬▬▬▬▬▬▬▬▬▬▬▬

John 13:1–20 ... what a beautiful passage from God's Word! Christ perfectly illustrates the obedience of a servant in this text. Let's observe it together.

- Reread John 13:1–20. Earlier in the study guide we used the method of *paraphrasing*. Let's utilize that method again in these twenty verses. Paraphrasing is writing out the verses in your own words in order to express the meaning of the words on the page. You're attempting to discover the feelings and thoughts that are displayed in this story. Begin with prayer. Ask God to show you something special in John 13, and believe that He will.

 Living Insights

Study Two ▬▬▬▬▬▬▬▬▬▬▬▬▬▬▬▬▬▬▬▬▬▬▬▬▬▬

Obedience means personal involvement prompted by unselfishness. It goes beyond mere business and activity. It's often hard work, but it is through obedience that we find ultimate happiness.

- This message is geared toward action! Christlike unselfishness involves living where *He* says and doing what *He* requires. How do you stack up? There are countless ways we can "wash one another's feet." Determine to make this servantlike obedience a way of life for you and immediately begin to *act* upon it! Seek the counsel of a friend, pastor, or church leader, and talk over your involvement

64

level. Allow this individual to aid you in suggesting possible options for involvement. Weigh them, discuss their pros and cons, and then make your decision! Use this chart to help you sort out your thoughts.

Ways in Which I Can Wash Another's Feet
1.
2.
3.
4.

Obedience Personified
Genesis 22

Obedience—it's an unpopular word, and it often conjures up images of a difficult and burdensome lifestyle. In the previous lesson, we saw obedience displayed in the life of Jesus and learned that it involves humility and gentleness. But what about those times when God asks us to do the uncomfortable, the painful, the sacrificial? We find that it isn't difficult to obey Him when our schedules aren't disrupted or our comforts are well taken care of. However, when obedience calls for great sacrifice—that's where we often draw the line. But that is a grave mistake! As we will discover from Abraham's experience, there are times when God does require sacrificial obedience from His own. And when we obey, He will generously reward us.

I. Revelation of the Test (Genesis 22:1–2)

The first words we read in this chapter are, "Now it came about after these things." When we read these words, we should ask ourselves, After what things? If you read chapters 12–21, you can learn of the events which had occurred in Abraham's life. Note, for example, his departure from his home, Ur of the Chaldeans, and all that was familiar to him; his bidding farewell to his favorite nephew, Lot, who went to live in Sodom and Gomorrah; and the birth of his son Isaac, the one through whom God promised to bring blessing to all of Abraham's descendants (17:9–21). After these and a number of other happenings, Abraham was confronted with his most difficult test:

> God tested Abraham, and said to him, "Abraham!" And he said, "Here I am." And He said, "Take now your son, your only son, whom you love, Isaac, and go to the land of Moriah; and offer him there as a burnt offering on one of the mountains of which I will tell you." (22:1b–2)

God targeted in on the son who had become first priority in Abraham's life, the one he dearly loved and who was the fruit of the promised future blessing. He instructed Abraham to offer Isaac up as an *olah,* "a whole burnt offering." But to accomplish this, Abraham had to travel with his son to the "land of Moriah," an arduous three-days' journey from their present location (cf. 22:4). Imagine traveling with your only son or daughter for three days and two nights, knowing all the while that at the end of the journey, *you* had to kill your child. Words cannot express the deep anguish Abraham must have felt when he heard God's words. And we can imply from verse 3 that he was so disturbed about the task ahead of him that he "rose early in the morning"—suggesting a sleepless night—and

"Obedience Personified" is in the cassette series but is not included in the book.

made all the travel preparations himself instead of delegating the job to his servants—another sign of his restlessness. Sure, Abraham acted in obedience to God's command, but this didn't negate the inner turmoil he experienced while carrying out the command.

II. **Response of Abraham** (Genesis 22:3–10)

Abraham's faith and obedience were now on the line. He had been requested by God to make a tremendous sacrifice. What would he do? What would *we* have done in such a situation? Would we have obeyed? The text has preserved for us what Abraham did in response to this demanding test:

> So Abraham rose early in the morning and saddled his donkey, and took two of his young men with him and Isaac his son; and he split wood for the burnt offering, and arose and went to the place of which God had told him. On the third day Abraham raised his eyes and saw the place from a distance. And Abraham said to his young men, "Stay here with the donkey, and I and the lad will go yonder; and we will worship and return to you." And Abraham took the wood of the burnt offering and laid it on Isaac his son, and he took in his hand the fire and the knife. So the two of them walked on together. And Isaac spoke to Abraham his father and said, "My father!" And he said, "Here I am, my son." And he said, "Behold, the fire and the wood, but where is the lamb for the burnt offering?" And Abraham said, "God will provide for Himself the lamb for the burnt offering, my son." So the two of them walked on together. Then they came to the place of which God had told him; and Abraham built the altar there, and arranged the wood, and bound his son Isaac, and laid him on the altar on top of the wood. And Abraham stretched out his hand, and took the knife to slay his son.

Let's stop here a moment and observe four key elements in Abraham's response.

A. It was marked by obedience (v. 3). Shortly after God gave the command, Abraham began to obey it. He made all the travel preparations, including the cutting of the wood for the burnt offering. There is no indication in the text that Abraham ever contemplated doing anything other than fulfilling the divine imperative he had received.

B. It was characterized by faith (vv. 4–6). Even though God had told Abraham that his promised son, Isaac, would be the sacrifice, Abraham never faltered in his faith. We can see this in verse 5: "And Abraham said to his young men, 'Stay here with the donkey, and I and the lad will go yonder; and *we will* worship and [*we will*] return to you' " (emphasis added). Abraham had no doubt that Isaac would return with him alive after the sacrifice. In the eleventh chapter of Hebrews, we read why Abraham could maintain such a conviction.

> By faith Abraham, when he was tested, offered up Isaac; and he who had received the promises was offering up his only begotten son; it was he to whom it was said, "In Isaac your descendants shall be called." He considered that God is able to raise men even from the dead; from which he also received him back as a type. (Heb. 11:17–19)

Abraham never let go of God's promise that Isaac would carry on his heritage. He knew that even if Isaac had to die, God was able to raise him to life again. No doubt this enabled him to walk side by side with his son who was carrying the wood for the offering (Gen. 22:6).

C. It was based on the character of God (vv. 7–8). As they were walking together, Isaac asked his father a very natural question: " 'Behold, the fire and the wood, but where is the lamb for the burnt offering?' " (v. 7b). Abraham's answer reflected his confidence in the faithfulness of God which he had experienced through the years: "And Abraham said, 'God will provide for Himself the lamb for the burnt offering, my son' " (v. 8a). He was still not sure how God would spare Isaac's life—whether it would be through providing another sacrifice or raising his son from the dead—but he continued to believe that God would provide for his needs and keep His promise concerning Isaac.

D. It was thorough and complete (vv. 9–10). When they finally reached their destination, "Abraham built the altar there, and arranged the wood, and bound his son Isaac, and laid him on the altar on top of the wood" (v. 9). Abraham followed God's orders completely; nothing was omitted. After everything was arranged and ready for the sacrifice, "Abraham stretched out his hand, and took the knife to slay his son" (v. 10).

III. Reward of God (Genesis 22:11–19)

As Abraham stood there, ready to plunge the knife into his own son, the angel of the Lord stopped him. Abraham had proven to be obedient and faithful to God. And God rewarded him by sparing his son's life and providing a substitute sacrifice: "Then Abraham raised his eyes and looked, and behold, behind him a ram caught in the thicket by his horns; and Abraham went and took the ram, and offered him up for a burnt offering in the place of his son" (v. 13). Abraham never stopped believing that God would provide. His faith in the Lord gave him the ability to carry out an incredible command

and thus to pass the test. So God left him with a blessing—an emphatic restatement of the promise He had made to him back in Genesis 15:5.

> "By Myself I have sworn, declares the Lord, because you have done this thing, and have not withheld your son, your only son, indeed I will greatly bless you, and I will greatly multiply your seed as the stars of the heavens, and as the sand which is on the seashore; and your seed shall possess the gate of their enemies. And in your seed all the nations of the earth shall be blessed, because you have obeyed My voice." (Gen. 22:16–18)

IV. Reminders for Us

No one ever said obedience was easy. In fact, it can be harder than disobedience. For obedience involves bending our own will to conform to God's will, and that entails the sacrifice of our selfishness. That's a difficult price to pay for self-centered people. But it's necessary for those of us who desire to be God's servants. Nothing can come before Him—not ourselves, our possessions, our dreams ... or even our own children. The story of Abraham's willingness to sacrifice his only son clearly illustrates that. There are three lessons embedded in this account that we need to remember.

A. What you retain for yourself is usually what God will ask you to release to Him. God is to be first in our lives—a position He jealously guards (cf. Deut. 6:5, 13–15). Whenever we exalt something else to the point of taking His place, we run the risk of having it taken from us.

B. What you release to God, He will replace with something better. As with Abraham, God can and may return to us what we release to Him. But if He chooses to retain what we have given into His hands, we may rest assured that He will replace it with something much better (cf. Job 42:10–17).

C. When God replaces, He also rewards. God blessed Abraham beyond his wildest dreams. And this was consistent with His all-good, just nature. God never fails to reward the sacrificial obedience of His people. So we can be confident that anything He may require of us will never compare to the unfathomable riches He will so abundantly lavish upon us as our reward.

Living Insights

Study One ▬▬▬▬▬▬▬▬▬▬▬▬▬▬▬▬▬

As was already stated, few tests hit harder than the tests related to one's children. If you are a parent, have you ever thought about what your reaction would be if God put the same test to you? Let's go a little further with that idea.

● Gather your family together around the Scriptures. Read aloud Genesis 22:1–19. Then read it aloud again from another translation or, preferably, a paraphrase. Finally, read it again, but this time substitute *your name* for Abraham's and *your children's names* for Isaac's. This should lead into a rather heavy discussion. Be frank, open, honest, and vulnerable. This conversation could make a memory for a lifetime. Close by holding hands and praying together.

 Living Insights

Study Two ▬▬▬▬▬▬▬▬▬▬▬▬▬▬▬▬▬

For many of us, the application of this lesson is difficult indeed. It deals with the "throne of our inner man." And that involves struggle—constant struggle. Here are some ways to work through these issues in a practical way.

● We have many things we hold dear to ourselves. The dearer they are, the more painful the release. What are you holding on to? This is a subject that is understandably difficult to consider. Silently sit for a time and ponder the significance of releasing your all to God.

● Perhaps putting things on paper would help to further clarify your thoughts. Record a list of the most important things in your life, such as your child, your job, your home, your reputation, your retirement, your cherished dreams. Now put a check (√) by the ones you've released to God. Circle any that remain. What will it take for you to give God the circled items? Jot down your thoughts.

● We can think and write about releasing … but still not release! However, by releasing, we allow God to reward us and replace what we give Him with something better. It all boils down to our ability to loosen our grip. Will you? Think about it, write about it, pray about it, and then take the final but necessary step … act upon it!

The Consequences of Serving

1 Peter 2–3; 2 Corinthians 4, 11

Reaching out is risky. Serving can backfire and burn you badly . . . deeply . . . painfully. How easy it is to get the false impression that once you are committed to assisting others, the blessings will fall upon you without stopping. Not so! There are definite and unique consequences that often accompany serving others. Authentic servants are not protected from the difficulties of their calling. As we shall see in this study, there are times when the struggles of servanthood are almost enough to cause a person to throw up his or her hands in frustration and give up.

I. A Realistic Appraisal of Serving (1 Peter 2:18–20, 3:17)

If we serve others long enough, it is inevitable that we will be mistreated for doing what is right. Often our giving, forgiving, forgetting, and obeying can result in misunderstanding, resentment, and even hostility. But it should not surprise us when we experience these kinds of reactions; they comprise the painful reality of servanthood, a fact not hidden from us in Scripture.

A. Suffering for doing what is right.

There is no passage in God's Word that shelters us from the reality of persecution and suffering. In fact, we are told many times that we should expect tribulation in our lives. But what should our response be when we suffer *unjustly*, when we are wronged for doing what is right? Peter's words in regard to this are very plain but difficult to accept. Let's take careful note of what he says:

> Servants, be submissive to your masters with all respect, not only to those who are good and gentle, but also to those who are unreasonable. For this finds favor, if for the sake of conscience toward God a man bears up under sorrows when suffering unjustly. For what credit is there if, when you sin and are harshly treated, you endure it with patience? But if when you do what is right and suffer for it you patiently endure it, this finds favor with God. (1 Pet. 2:18–20)

Peter even goes on to say that "it is better, if God should will it so, that you suffer for doing what is right rather than for doing what is wrong" (3:17). Why? Because God uses unfair circumstances in our lives to break our strong, stubborn wills so He can mold us into the likeness of His Son, Jesus Christ. Through our experience of unjust pain and affliction, we are perfected by God just as Christ was through the undeserved sufferings He endured—even to His death on a cross for *our* sins (cf. Heb. 2:10, 5:8–9; 1 Pet. 2:20–24, 3:17–18).

71

B. Responding to treatment that is wrong. Bitterness often comes when we have been disillusioned through mistreatment. But we should understand that throughout history ill-treatment has often followed on the heels of right actions. Many of us have read accounts in Scripture and have heard the testimonies of innumerable Christians who have been ridiculed, slandered, threatened, tortured, even killed, simply for living out their Christian faith. The question is not, Will we as Christians ever be unjustly maligned? but, How should we respond when we are treated unfairly? That's what we want to discover in this lesson: How we can endure mistreatment so as to avoid the paralyzing sting of bitterness and disillusionment, and thus bring glory to God.

II. The Dark Side of Serving (2 Corinthians 4:4, 7–9)

In this passage, Paul helps us to maintain a proper perspective on our suffering. He first reminds us that we are merely "earthen vessels," that is, clay pots filled with the treasure of God's message (vv. 4, 7). Why has God placed such a priceless treasure in such frail, perishable containers? So "that the surpassing greatness of the power may be of God and not from ourselves" (v. 7b), answers Paul. We are insufficient in ourselves to accomplish the tasks God has given us. But that's as He designed it. For in this way none can doubt that the power to do God's will comes from Him and Him alone. And just so we never forget this truth, God allows certain struggles or consequences to enter into the lives of His servants. We need to know what they are so that we can better handle them when they come. Let's look at them together: "We are *afflicted* in every way, but not crushed; *perplexed,* but not despairing; *persecuted,* but not forsaken; *struck down,* but not destroyed" (vv. 8–9, emphasis added).

A. Affliction. The Greek word for this term is *thlíbo.* It means "to subject to pressure, to afflict." It refers to the harassment, oppression, and tribulation that servants feel when they experience difficult circumstances or antagonistic people.

B. Confusion. There are times when we all feel "perplexed." These occasions are characterized by feelings of disillusionment and insecurity. There may even be moments when we doubt God.

C. Persecution. The word *driven* is a good synonym for the original Greek term in this verse. It's an aggressive, active word which means "to set somebody on the run, to put to flight, to hunt down like an animal." God's servants *will* be persecuted; they are not exempt.

D. Rejection. This fourth word translated *struck down* carries the idea of being shoved aside or cast off. Paul warns us that even though we may be faithful in doing our God-given tasks, there will come times when we will be deserted and rejected.

III. Spelling Out the Consequences (2 Corinthians 11:23–28)

In Paul's life we see an amplified example of his own words. During numerous occasions he suffered affliction, confusion, persecution, and rejection. In fact, he begins this section of his letter with the question, "Are they servants of Christ?" In some ways his following answer is surprising. He does not capitalize on his service or on all the good works he has performed, though he could easily have done both. Rather, he spells out the times of suffering and hardship he experienced, showing that he has a better claim on servanthood than others.

> Are they servants of Christ? (I speak as if insane) I more so; in far more labors, in far more imprisonments, beaten times without number, often in danger of death. Five times I received from the Jews thirty-nine lashes. Three times I was beaten with rods, once I was stoned, three times I was shipwrecked, a night and a day I have spent in the deep. I have been on frequent journeys, in dangers from rivers, dangers from robbers, dangers from my countrymen, dangers from the Gentiles, dangers in the city, dangers in the wilderness, dangers on the sea, dangers among false brethren; I have been in labor and hardship, through many sleepless nights, in hunger and thirst, often without food, in cold and exposure. Apart from such external things, there is the daily pressure upon me of concern for all the churches. (2 Cor. 11:23–28)

A. In labors. Paul knew what it meant to be afflicted. He faced the pressure, personal toil, and trouble that go with ministry and authentic servanthood. There were probably many nights he could not sleep because of his concern for the churches. In addition, there were numerous occasions when he went without food, warmth, and adequate housing (vv. 27–28). Very few of us can even begin to imagine what it would be like to live through this kind of affliction, and even fewer of us would be willing to live a life that was characterized by such suffering. But Paul saw these things as marks of his servanthood—all strong signs that he was faithfully being and doing what God desired.

B. In imprisonments. These were experiences of confusion and disillusionment for Paul. He described them eight times in verse 26 by using the Greek word *kíndunos,* which is translated "danger." He was threatened, pushed around, intimidated, and treated unfairly—all for doing what was right! Times like these can bring on a disoriented state of mind that imprisons a person with unanswered questions and doubts. But God is gracious with His servants during such experiences. He will provide them with the strength they need to victoriously endure.

C. **In beatings.** In times of persecution, Paul suffered beatings without number. He recalled some specific cases of those beatings: "Five times I received . . . thirty-nine lashes. Three times I was beaten with rods, once I was stoned" (vv. 24–25a). But even through occasions of great physical abuse, Paul regarded his mistreatment as a consequence of his faithful service.

D. **In danger of death.** With such a list, we would think that Paul had experienced enough, but there is one more category of sufferings he recounts: the danger of death itself. He knew what it was like to be hungry, thirsty, cold, shipwrecked, stranded in the ocean, and stoned. And remember, he went through all this and more as one who was innocent of doing any wrong. He was hated for doing what was right, not for what was wrong. The same treatment is inflicted upon authentic servants today.

IV. Suggestions for Coping with the Consequences

At times questions of fairness are completely irrelevant. What really matters is not so much whether a situation is fair or not, but what our attitude and response is in the midst of it all. We have been warned that if we are faithful in serving Christ, we can expect to be mistreated. What we need to decide, then, is what our response will be when ill-treatment comes. The wrong response can dishonor God and cause us to become bitter. However, if we focus on God's grace and maintain a proper perspective, we can better cope with these horrible consequences. There are two further important truths which can also help us.

A. **Nothing touches me that has not passed through the hands of my Heavenly Father.** It's important to remember that even when things are the darkest, God is still in control.

B. **Everything I endure is designed to prepare me for serving others more effectively.** Our times of testing are meant to purify us. They also make us better equipped to serve and minister to others when they are faced with similar struggles and trials.

 Living Insights

It's always important to present topics in a context of *realism*. Thus, in speaking of servanthood, there is a "backwash" to servanthood that is painful. This study may hurt, but it is necessary.

● Eight words or phrases are briefly developed in this lesson. Identify the one or ones which most closely relate to your situation. With the assistance of your Bible and concordance, conduct a topical study on those specific words or phrases. Seek to glean all you can from the Scriptures on each subject. Begin by asking God for His help.

—Affliction
—Confusion
—Persecution
—Rejection

—In Labors
—In Imprisonments
—In Beatings
—In Danger of Death

 Living Insights

Study Two ▬▬▬▬▬▬▬▬▬▬▬▬▬▬▬▬▬▬▬

Do I really believe that suffering for doing right is best? Am I willing to accept this as God's will? Can I patiently endure in order to please God? How does Christ's suffering compare with what I am going through?

- Take the following two truths and write each of them on a separate page of your notebook. Now, in the context of difficult circumstances, what do these statements mean to you? Write down some of your personal feelings concerning each sentence. Be honest. Pour out your heart to God.

    —*Nothing* touches me that has not passed through the hands of my Heavenly Father.

    —*Everything* I endure is designed to prepare me for serving others more effectively.

The Rewards of Serving

Selected Scripture

Make no mistake about it, not one act of service done in the name of the Lord Jesus Christ will go unnoticed or unrewarded. As we shall see, those rewards may not all occur in this lifetime—in fact, *most won't*—but neither will they be forgotten. Our God honors every action that stems from an unselfish motive, and He will see to it that each one receives its proper and sufficient reward. Servants, take heart! Whether it be eternal crowns or earthly benefits, your God is faithful to remember authentic servanthood. Stay at the task of ministering. The rewards will ultimately overshadow all the perils and consequences you experienced while serving Him. In times like these, we need that encouraging reminder.

I. Biblical Facts about Rewards (1 Corinthians 3:10–14)

We live in a reward-oriented society. Even many church hymns speak of heavenly rewards and crowns. But what does Scripture have to say on this subject? Let's look at the passage given above and note three things that it reveals about rewards—specifically, those awarded by God to His servants for their faithfulness and obedience.

A. Most rewards will be received in heaven, not on earth (vv. 13–14).

We are trained to look for our rewards in the present rather than in the future. So it's easy for us to get caught in the trap of wanting our rewards immediately. But this expectation is not altogether biblical. Many of our rewards will be revealed to us in heaven when we stand before Christ. Then He will test our works with fire to determine their value. All that remains after this testing will warrant a reward.

B. All rewards are based on quality, not quantity (v. 13b).

Notice the last words of this verse: "And the fire itself will test the *quality* of each man's work" (emphasis added). We are often enamored with the size and physical appearance of a group, church, or individual ministry. But God does not judge a ministry on the basis of quantity. Instead, His assessment is founded on the motives and rationale behind any given ministry or act of service. And because He is omniscient, His knowledge of these things is complete and infallible.

C. No reward that is postponed will be forgotten (v. 14).

We are assured that "if any man's work which he has built upon it [namely, the foundation of Jesus Christ, v. 11] remains [after being tested by fire], *he shall receive a reward*" (emphasis added). Not a single act done in His name and power will go unrewarded, no matter how uncelebrated or obscure it might be. And even though we may become anxious and want our rewards now, we can be assured that our Lord will keep His promise to reward us for our faithful service, though He may wait until we reach heaven to do so.

II. God's Promises to His Servants

Someone has said that there are nearly 7,500 promises contained in the Scriptures. These promises could be categorized into two groups: those dealing with God's faithfulness and those dealing with our faithfulness. Let's briefly examine each of these categories.

A. Regarding His faithfulness. The whole reward system that God has established starts with His faithfulness. Oftentimes we have little more to hang onto than the promises of God, all of which depend on His faithfulness to fulfill them. But what does it mean to say that God is faithful? Two points stand out. First, *He is steadfast in His affection and His allegiance to His people.* Unlike many people, God can never be accused of being fickle or abandoning His followers. The prophet Isaiah records this truth in these comforting words:

" 'Do not fear, for I am with you;
Do not anxiously look about you, for I am your God.
I will strengthen you, surely I will help you,
Surely I will uphold you with
　My righteous right hand.' " (Isa. 41:10)
But Zion said, "The Lord has forsaken me,
And the Lord has forgotten me.
Can a woman forget her nursing child,
And have no compassion on the son of her womb?
Even these may forget, but I will not forget you.
Behold, I have inscribed you on the palms of
　My hands;
Your walls are continually before Me." (Isa. 49:14–16)

Second, *He is firm in His adherence to His promises.* If He says that He will do something, then we can depend on Him to do it. He always keeps His word. And just so we won't forget this fact, even in times of doubt, the writer of Hebrews penned this verse:

> For God is not unjust so as to forget your work and the love which you have shown toward His name, in having ministered and in still ministering to the saints. (Heb. 6:10)

Please note: This passage tells us that there are two things God faithfully remembers about His servants: (1) their work and (2) the love within them that prompts it. God keeps a dependable, accurate record of the works which we do. And He also takes into account the motive behind each work, whether it is done out of love for others or a desire to exalt self.

B. Regarding our faithfulness. Several passages in the New Testament speak of God's promises to His faithful servants. In these words we find that some rewards are temporal while others are eternal.

1. **Temporal rewards** (2 Cor. 4:7–11). There is a painful part of serving, and this passage displays that for us. But this text also indicates that our earthly rewards can come through even the toughest experiences of serving. Indeed, says Paul, the scars and wounds received from doing Christ's work actually reveal His life (vv. 10–11). From this section of Scripture we may discern two rewards that are manifested through even the dark side of serving. The first is *the quiet awareness that the life of Christ is being modeled before others.* And the second is *the joyful realization that a thankful spirit is being stimulated in others.* When being a servant seems thankless and unnoticed, remember these rewards. They will help you to recall that serving is never insignificant or unprofitable.

2. **Eternal rewards.** Paul tells us that there will be a day when we shall all stand "before the judgment seat of Christ, that each one may be recompensed for his deeds in the body" (2 Cor. 5:10). At that time Christians will receive eternal rewards for their earthly works. These will be in addition to some of the temporal rewards we have already examined. During this heavenly award ceremony, we who are Christians will hear our Lord's own words: " 'Well done, good and faithful slave; . . . enter into the joy of your master' " (Matt. 25:23). That is when we will know the fullness of His grace and be ushered into a state of everlasting joy with God. We will also receive crowns (or rewards). There are at least five eternal crowns spoken of in the New Testament: (1) *the imperishable crown* (1 Cor. 9:24–27) is promised to those who victoriously run the race of life; (2) *the crown of exultation* (Phil. 4:1, 1 Thess. 2:19–20) will be given to those who were faithful in declaring the gospel, leading people to Christ, and building them up in Him; (3) *the crown of righteousness* (2 Tim. 4:7–8) will be awarded to those who live in anticipation of Christ's coming; (4) *the crown of life* (James 1:12) awaits those who have suffered for Christ in their earthly life; and (5) *the crown of glory* (1 Pet. 5:1–4) is promised to those who faithfully minister the Word. Now in heaven His servants will not boast over these crowns or hoard them. Rather, Revelation 4 reveals that they will cast their crowns at Jesus' feet and bow in worship of Him. Furthermore, unlike earthly awards and trophies that, once

won, are soon forgotten and eventually waste away, the crowns we will receive will last throughout eternity, never to be forgotten, tarnished, or ruined. They will be everlasting reminders of God's grace and faithfulness toward us.

III. Encouragement to Servants

We've covered a lot of territory in this series on servanthood. And we have seen that the life to which we are called is not an easy one. In fact, it can be just plain hard work! But we have also seen that Christ has not left us to grope our way along in uncertainty and despair. He has given us His example to teach us, His Spirit to guide us, and His power to enable us. What a complete survival and victory kit! And to top it all off, He has promised that He will reward us for our faithfulness. When we contemplate this and all that we have covered, we discover three truths we should embrace and constantly keep before us.

A. **Every act of servanthood will be remembered and rewarded by God.** No matter how small or how large, God takes note of every act His servants do and will one day reward them abundantly.

B. **He takes special note of the heart.** He is not impressed by the size of the act but by the motive of love behind it.

C. **A servant's heart remains the rarest gem on earth.** Unfortunately, few of us truly possess a servant's heart. But it is not unattainable for one who has trusted in Christ for his or her salvation. If you have not done this, then do it now—don't wait! If you have accepted the salvation Christ offers, then get going with His plan of sanctification called servanthood. He has given you all you need. The only thing He can't do is be a servant for you—you must actively engage in that yourself. He will help and encourage you in every way possible, but without your willful participation in the process, it *cannot* occur. The price of serving is high, for it demands that you turn your whole life over to Christ. But the rewards far exceed the cost you will have to pay. So if you haven't already, launch out on the road of servanthood. Become a rare breed. You will not regret it!

Living Insights

Study One ▄▄▄▄▄▄▄▄▄▄▄▄▄▄▄▄▄▄▄▄▄▄▄▄▄▄▄▄

Due to your interaction with this series, is it fair to say you'll be improving your serve? Let's pause to review where we've been in this study. What did you *learn* in this series?

● Copy the following chart into your notebook. Next to each message title, write down the most important truth you discovered from that particular lesson. Feel free to page through your Bible, study guide, and notebook.

Improving Your Serve	
Message Titles	Important Truths
Who, Me a Servant? You Gotta Be Kidding!	
God's Work, My Involvement	
A Case for Unselfishness	
The Servant as a Giver	
The Servant as a Forgiver	
The Servant as a Forgetter	
Thinking like a Servant Thinks	
Portrait of a Servant (Part One)	
Portrait of a Servant (Part Two)	
The Influence of a Servant	
The Perils of a Servant	
The Obedience of a Servant	
Obedience Personified	
The Consequences of Serving	
The Rewards of Serving	

 *Living Insights*

What we learn in a series is important, but what we *apply* is crucial. Let's turn our attention toward application. How have you *changed* as a result of this series?

- Copy the following chart into your notebook. Repeat the same process as in study one; however, in this review look for the meaningful applications that were made as a result of each message.

Improving Your Serve	
Message Titles	Meaningful Applications
Who, Me a Servant? You Gotta Be Kidding!	
God's Work, My Involvement	
A Case for Unselfishness	
The Servant as a Giver	
The Servant as a Forgiver	
The Servant as a Forgetter	
Thinking like a Servant Thinks	
Portrait of a Servant (Part One)	
Portrait of a Servant (Part Two)	
The Influence of a Servant	
The Perils of a Servant	
The Obedience of a Servant	
Obedience Personified	
The Consequences of Serving	
The Rewards of Serving	

Books for Probing Further

Although few books fully treat the subject of Christian servanthood, there are several good books that deal with various aspects of an authentic servant's life. Some of the better sources are given below. We would encourage you to use these tools for the purpose of probing further into how a true servant can and should live. But remember, Christ's servants are to apply His truth, not merely learn it. So use these tools to further aid you in appropriation, not just education.

I. Books on Servant Living
These will give you more help for living a life of consistent holiness and purity.

Aldrich, Joe. *Secrets to Inner Beauty: Transforming Life through Love.* Foreword by Howard Hendricks. Portland: Multnomah Press, 1977.

Bridges, Jerry. *The Practice of Godliness.* The Christian Character Library. Colorado Springs: NavPress, 1983.

Bridges, Jerry. *The Pursuit of Holiness.* Colorado Springs: NavPress, 1978.

Grounds, Vernon. *Radical Commitment: Getting Serious about Christian Growth.* Portland: Multnomah Press, 1984.

Lewis, C. S. *The Screwtape Letters.* New York: Macmillan Publishing Co., Inc., 1977.

Lutzer, Erwin W. *How to Say No to a Stubborn Habit—Even When You Feel Like Saying Yes.* Foreword by Stuart Briscoe. Wheaton: Victor Books, 1979.

MacDonald, Gordon. *Ordering Your Private World.* Nashville: Thomas Nelson Publishers, 1984.

Schaeffer, Francis A. *True Spirituality.* Wheaton: Tyndale House Publishers, 1971.

Swindoll, Charles R. *Killing Giants, Pulling Thorns.* Foreword by Senator Mark O. Hatfield. Portland: Multnomah Press, 1978.

Swindoll, Charles R. *Moral Purity.* Fullerton: Insight for Living, 1985.

Swindoll, Charles R. *Strengthening Your Grip: Essentials in an Aimless World.* Waco: Word Books, 1982.

White, John. *The Fight: A Practical Handbook for Christian Living.* Downers Grove: InterVarsity Press, 1976.

II. Books on Servant Reaching
These will focus your attention on how to touch the lives of others, whether they be Christians or non-Christians.

Aldrich, Joseph C. *Life-style Evangelism: Crossing Traditional Boundaries to Reach the Unbelieving World.* A Critical Concern Book. Portland: Multnomah Press, 1981.

Cocoris, G. Michael. *Evangelism: A Biblical Approach.* Foreword by Haddon Robinson. Chicago: Moody Press, 1984.

Hendricks, Howard G. *Say It with Love.* Wheaton: Victor Books, 1972.

Hull, Bill. *Jesus Christ Disciplemaker.* Foreword by Joe Aldrich. Colorado Springs: NavPress, 1984.

MacDonald, Gail and Gordon. *If Those Who Reach Could Touch.* Nashville: Thomas Nelson Publishers, 1984.

Swindoll, Charles R. *Dropping Your Guard: The Value of Open Relationships.* Waco: Word Books, 1983.

Swindoll, Chuck. *Compassion.* Lifemaps series. Waco: Word Books, 1984.

III. Books on Servant Thinking

In our day we desperately need Christians who can think and act from a thoroughly Christian mind-set. The following books will guide you toward this essential goal.

Barclay, Oliver R. *The Intellect and Beyond.* Grand Rapids: Academie Books, Zondervan Publishing House, 1985.

Blamires, Harry. *The Christian Mind: How Should a Christian Think?* Ann Arbor: Servant Books, 1978; first published, 1963.

Stott, John R. W. *Your Mind Matters: The Place of the Mind in the Christian Life.* Downers Grove: InterVarsity Press, 1972.

Swindoll, Charles R. *Make Up Your Mind . . . about the Issues of Life.* Portland: Multnomah Press, 1981.

Woodbridge, John D., ed. *Renewing Your Mind in a Secular World.* Chicago: Moody Press, 1985.

IV. Books on Servant Leading

You cannot be the kind of leader God desires until you start to become a leader with a servant's heart. These works can give you the necessary biblical direction toward servant leading.

Barber, Cyril. *Nehemiah and the Dynamics of Effective Leadership.* Neptune: Loizeaux Brothers, 1976.

Barber, Cyril J., and Strauss, Gary H. *Leadership: The Dynamics of Success.* Foreword by Dr. Vernon C. Grounds. Greenwood: The Attic Press, 1982.

Eims, LeRoy. *Be the Leader You Were Meant to Be.* Foreword by Theodore H. Epp. Wheaton: Victor Books, 1975.

Sanders, J. Oswald. *Paul the Leader.* Colorado Springs: NavPress, 1984.

Swindoll, Charles R. *Hand Me Another Brick.* Nashville: Thomas Nelson Publishers, 1978.

Swindoll, Chuck. *Leadership.* Lifemaps series. Waco: Word Books, 1985.

V. Books on Servant Suffering

As Christ's servants, we will experience pain and suffering. How can we handle it? How should we act through it? How can we help others who hurt? These books will provide you with answers to these questions and many others.

Baker, Don. *Pain's Hidden Purpose: Finding Perspective in the Midst of Suffering.* Portland: Multnomah Press, 1984.

Lewis, C. S. *The Problem of Pain.* New York: Macmillan Publishing Co., Inc., 1962.

Swindoll, Chuck. *For Those Who Hurt.* Portland: Multnomah Press, 1977.

Wiersbe, Warren W. *Why Us? When Bad Things Happen to God's People.* Old Tappan: Fleming H. Revell Co., 1984.

Yancey, Philip. *Where Is God When It Hurts?* Grand Rapids: Zondervan Publishing House; Wheaton: Campus Life Books, 1977.